HEALTHY LIFESTYLES 3

SPHE ACTIVITIES FOR THIRD YEAR STUDENTS

Edel O'Brien
Róisín Moore

Gill & Macmillan

Gill & Macmillan Ltd
Hume Avenue
Park West
Dublin 12
with associated companies throughout the world
www.gillmacmillan.ie

978 0 7171 4246 0

Print origination in Ireland by Outburst Design

The paper used in this book is made from the wood pulp of managed forests. For every tree felled, at least one tree is planted, thereby renewing natural resources.

For permission to reproduce the photograph on page 122, the author and publisher gratefully acknowledge © Photocall.

Contents

Module 1

Belonging and Integrating

Goal Setting for Third Years

A goal is something worth putting effort into achieving. It is a purpose or target. In the modern world all successful organisations and individuals set targets for themselves.

List some individuals or groups who you think might set goals for themselves.

Name of individual / group	Goal
Republic of Ireland soccer team	To qualify for the next World Cup
Local shop	To sell a specific number of newspapers every day

Use some old magazines and newspapers to make a collage or draw images representing your goals for the future and the things you hope to accomplish in your life. Include in your collage/drawing the things you would like to have, the things you would like to achieve, the lifestyle you would like to have, etc.

Discuss your collage/images with a partner and examine in what ways your goals/aims are different and in what ways they are similar.

1

Differences	Similarities
_____	_____
_____	_____
_____	_____

The beginning of the year is a good time to focus yourself and set your goals. When setting goals try to be SMART!

- **S**pecific
- **M**easurable
- **A**ction-related
- **R**ealistic
- **T**ime-based.

 # Specific

Don't have as a goal something like 'to be good at basketball'. Instead make your target 'to improve from scoring five baskets out of twenty to scoring ten baskets out of twenty'.

 # Measurable

Record your improvements so that you can see your progress as you move towards your goal. Keep a checklist of the chapters you need to study and tick them off as you revise each one.

 # Action-related

Break down your task into a set of steps and put your efforts into achieving one of these steps rather than tackling all of them at once.

Someone training for the marathon does not go out the first day and try to run 26 miles in four hours. They might aim to start by running two miles and gradually increase their distance.

 # Realistic

You are destined to fail if your goal is unrealistic to begin with. Ask someone with experience in the area whether what you are attempting to do is achievable.

Deciding that you are never going to fight with your younger brother is unrealistic, but making an effort to deal with your anger better is realistic.

Time-based

Make sure you allow enough time to achieve your aim. Deciding to practise the piano a week before your exam is unlikely to yield great results.

What are your targets for the year?

_____

_____

_____

Personal	Health
Academic	Home life
Leisure	And ...?

Goals aren't easy to achieve and it is best to plan.

Premiership soccer clubs have to examine their strengths and weaknesses at the start of the season and buy players in order to achieve their targets. Their plans are geared towards achieving the goal of finishing as high as possible in the league.

Formula One teams make adjustments according to weather conditions, etc. In their plans they must allow time to practise pit stops and tyre changes in order to achieve pole position.

In order for you to achieve your goals you must make adjustments to your life. What simple steps can you take to enable you to achieve your goals?

_____

_____

_____

_____

What difficulties do you expect to face in trying to achieve your goals?

_____

_____

Do you think your goals are worth the effort? Why?

_____

_____

Remember to review your goals regularly!

Weekly Task

1 Write down your goals somewhere you can see them regularly. This will keep you motivated.

2 Make a list of your goals, put it in an envelope, seal the envelope and give it to a parent. At the end of the year ask for the envelope back and see how many goals you have achieved.

3 Discuss your goals with someone at home. They may be willing to help you achieve them.

Work Contract

 ## School mission statement

A school mission statement outlines the aims of the school and describes the type of education it tries to provide for all its students.

Read your school's mission statement.

What are the aims of your school?

_____

_____

_____

_____

Does the mission statement imply that the school aims to provide a broad education for the students? If so, one of the ways your school tries to achieve this is through SPHE: **S**ocial, **P**ersonal and **H**ealth **E**ducation. In SPHE you may not have to remember dates, theorems or definitions but you are still learning really important things.

 ## Individual Work

Can you think of any relevant or important information/skills you have learned in SPHE?

_____

_____

'SPHE class is a little bit different from other classes.' Do you agree with this statement?

_____

In what way is SPHE class different?

_____

_____

The things I have enjoyed in SPHE in first and second year are:

_____

_____

I dislike SPHE when:

_____

_____

_____

Perhaps you could discus your answers with other students.

Most groups have ground rules that their members are asked to agree to and abide by. In school you have a code of behaviour and classroom rules.

In SPHE class you have probably noticed that you work in groups, complete individual work, use meditation, role plays and discussion groups a lot more than in other subjects. Because of this your class may have to develop a specific set of guidelines on behaviour that's appropriate for SPHE classes.

Individual Task

What would help the class run well? _____

_____

What kind of behaviour prevents the class running well?_____

_____

What ground rules would you put in place to make sure the SPHE class runs smoothly?

_____

Group Task

Discuss your ideas with the group.

Perhaps others in the group have similar or different views from you. Try to come to an agreement over the ground rules the group would like to implement. Write the agreed ground rules here.

_____

_____

_____

One of your group may be asked to share the group's ideas with the rest of the class. The class as a whole must now try to agree to a set of guidelines. Remember: this also includes the teacher. Once everyone in the class has agreed on the guidelines you could design a poster/banner/collage to hang on the wall at the start of each class.

Write the class's agreed guidelines here and ask all your classmates to sign underneath to show that they support the guidelines.

_____

_____

_____

_____

_____

_____

_____

_____

_____

Signatures:

It might be necessary to review the guidelines regularly to make sure that everyone still agrees with them.

Module Review

Date:

In this module I learned about: _____

_____

I enjoyed this module because: _____

I disliked this module because: _____

I would rate this module __ out of ten for relevance to my life. This module was relevant/not relevant to my life because:

_____

_____

_____

Module 2

Self-Management: A Sense of Purpose

 Organising My Time

During the coming year you will probably find that school work and preparation for exams places a big demand on your time. It is important to manage your time well. In addition to homework you will probably have a number of projects, practical exams, portfolios and reports to complete. Unless you plan for these you will find that towards the end of the year you have lots of work and not very much time.

Below are some of the subjects for which you may have assignments, projects, portfolios or practical exams. Fill in the details for each subject.

Subject	Assignment	Due date	Percentage	Duration
CSPE				
Woodwork				
Religious Education				
Metalwork				
Technology				
Science				
Home Economics				
Art				
Music				

 Devising a Timetable

1 Set realistic goals for yourself.

2 If your exam results are important to you, be willing to make sacrifices throughout the year. Good results are achieved by consistent effort, not by cramming at the end.

3 Make a list of all your commitments, chores, favourite TV programmes, approximate mealtimes etc.

4 Make sure you allow enough time for homework in your study plan.

5 Do difficult homework first when you have more energy.

6 If you get stuck with something, try to work it out as best you can, but don't spend too much time on it or you will mess up your study timetable.

7 Your environment is really important. You need a quiet space with a comfortable chair and a desk or table large enough for your books. Try to keep all your stationery nearby so you don't have to go and look for things. Remove any items likely to distract you — magazines, mirror, posters, PlayStation etc.

8 Turn off your mobile phone and internet.

9 Some students find that music helps block out background noise, but if you find yourself getting distracted or reading the same page twice, turn off the music. And remember: your study conditions should be similar to exam conditions.

10 Devise a system of rewarding yourself. Discuss this with your parent/guardian. They may surprise you!

11 Review your timetable regularly.

It might be easier to draw up a timetable for someone else first. Have a go at drawing up a schedule for Suzanne.

Suzanne

Suzanne is a third-year student. She has decided to draw up a study timetable for the year. She has a busy social life and enjoys her leisure time with friends and family. Suzanne's day usually begins around 7.45 and she leaves the house at 8.30 to walk to school. School finishes at 3.45 and on Monday, Tuesday and Thursday she does supervised study in school from four o'clock until six. (On Wednesday she goes to dance class.) She normally gets most of her written work done in study time but finds it difficult to concentrate in the large hall.

She gets home at around 6.30 and has finished her dinner and tidied up by 7.30. Her favourite TV programmes are on from 9.30 to 10.30 on Tuesdays and Thursdays. On Friday Suzanne walks home from school with her friends and doesn't get home until 5.00. Normally she goes to the pool with her family from 6.00 to 7.30. After her dinner she usually goes babysitting for a few hours.

Saturday is her favourite day: she stays in bed until 11.00 and then goes to her dance class until 1.00. In the afternoon she hangs out with friends in town or goes to the cinema in the evening. Sunday is always spent lazing around or visiting her Nan and by Sunday afternoon she is exhausted and in no mood to study.

Can you draw up a study plan for Suzanne following the guidelines given above? She has 11 subjects for her Junior Certificate.

Time	Monday	Tuesday	Wednesday	Thursday	Friday	Saturday	Sunday

Compare your timetable with a partner and discuss any differences between
the two versions.

Colm

Colm is fifteen years old and attends his local community
school. There is a big emphasis on sport both in school and
at home. His parents have always encouraged him to
participate. Colm is a talented sportsman and is involved
with many of the school teams and a number of local
teams. His commitment to club and school takes up a lot of
time and between all his activities he has something on
every day after school and most weekends. He really
enjoys the activities as most of his friends are also involved.

Colm has started to get into trouble at school for not completing his homework and
for presenting untidy work. He is having a lot of difficulty with maths in particular as he
sometimes misses this class when he goes to school matches. He is frustrated because he
genuinely tries his best. However, Colm realises his sports are taking up a lot of his time
and he often feels tired. He is worried that his school work has suffered and that he
may not do as well as he had hoped in his Junior Certificate. His goal is to go to
college and then join his dad's business. He knows his parents would be really
disappointed if he didn't do well in school, but they would be equally disappointed if he
gave up sport. Colm feels under pressure.

Identify the issues facing Colm.

_____

What should Colm do?

_____

Where could Colm go for advice?

_____

Is it possible to balance extra-curricular activity and study?

_____

_____

What is the recommended study time for third-year students in your school?

_____

Weekly Task

1 Draw up a study timetable for yourself, keeping in mind the guidelines given on page 10.

Time	Monday	Tuesday	Wednesday	Thursday	Friday	Saturday	Sunday

2 Record all your practical work deadlines on a calendar at home so that you don't forget about them. If your family see that you are busy with portfolios, projects etc. you might find they are more supportive.

3 Record all your deadlines in your school journal or homework diary.

Planning for Effective Study

→ **Effective Study**

Have you ever spent an hour studying and then wondered what you have actually learned? Do you often find yourself reading the same page for 20 minutes? Do you feel that despite your efforts you seem to be getting nowhere?

Effective study is a skill — a skill that can be learned. The key is quality rather than quantity. Here are some tips to help with study. Your teacher and guidance counsellor will probably be able to give you some more, which you can jot down at the end.

1 Organise yourself. Make a list of the chapters that you need to cover and mark off each one as you revise it.

2 Study for 45 minutes and then take a 15-minute break. Sitting for long periods without stretching causes us to become less productive.

3 During your break try to get outside or at least get a change of scenery – walk the dog, kick a football, practise your basketball skills or call a friend. But don't make your break any longer than 15 minutes.

4 Get enough sleep. In a scientific study it was found that students who got a good night's sleep did better than those who stayed up all night studying.

5 Diet is also important. Believe it or not, eating breakfast plays an important part in helping you concentrate. Don't skip it!

6 Many Junior Certificate subjects include projects and practical work as well as exams. Make sure you write the deadlines and exam dates on a calendar so that they don't sneak up on you.

7 When you're reading through a chapter make a note of key ideas by highlighting them and jotting them down on a sheet of paper. This sheet of paper will then become part of your revision notes. You don't need to use full sentences, just lists and bullet points.

8 As you read through a chapter in school, highlight or underline important details. This will speed up your note-taking later.

9 Paying attention during class will save hours of study at home.

10 Make notes or mind maps of important points. These will help you to study closer to exam time.

11 Use rhymes and mnemonics to remember things. You probably know one for the colours of the rainbow (red, orange, yellow, green, blue, indigo and violet): Richard Of York Gave Battle In Vain. These are really useful if you have a list of terms to remember.

12 _____
   _____

13 _____
   _____

14 _____
   _____

Mind Mapping

A mind map is like a spider diagram that links the main ideas of a topic. It is very useful for revision. On the right is an example of a mind map for a topic in science.

Different people will draw mind maps slightly differently. Try to complete a mind map for a topic from one of your favourite subjects. If you share your mind map with friends you will have made a great study aid for your exams.

 # Mnemonics or Rhymes

It is often helpful to use triggers to remind us of important information. Even when we were younger we might have used a song to help us remember the alphabet, and rhymes for the days of the week and the numbers of days in each month of the year. Mnemonics and rhymes are really useful to help us remember a list of items or two similar pieces of information.

Many of you probably use 'Silly old Harry caught a herring trawling off America' to remember important information in trigonometry (sin, cos and tan). With a friend, try to devise mnemonics for the following lists from your science course.

1 **Nutrients**: carbohydrates, fats, proteins, vitamins and minerals.

_____

_____

2 **Planets**: Mercury, Venus, Earth, Mars, Jupiter, Saturn, Uranus, Neptune, Pluto.

_____

_____

3 **Characteristics of life**: movement, respiration, sensitivity, feeding, excretion, reproduction, growth.

_____

Can you think of anywhere else to use mnemonics or rhymes?

_____

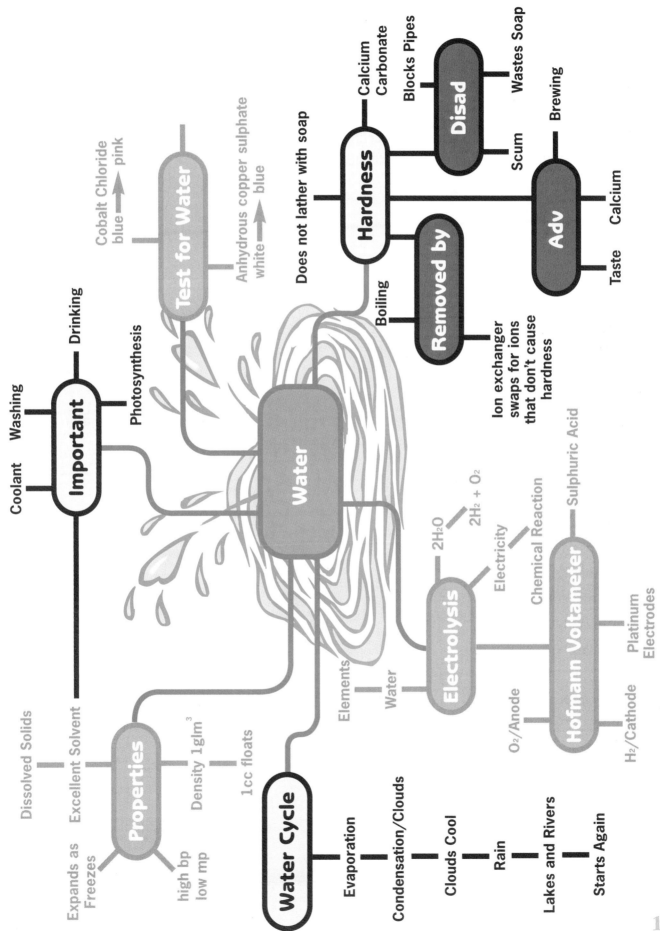

Water

Important
- Coolant
- Washing
- Drinking
- Photosynthesis

Test for Water
- Cobalt Chloride blue → pink
- Anhydrous copper sulphate white → blue

Hardness
- Does not lather with soap
- Calcium Carbonate
- Blocks Pipes
- **Disad**
  - Scum
  - Wastes Soap
- **Adv**
  - Brewing
  - Calcium
  - Taste
- Boiling
- **Removed by**
- Ion exchanger swaps for ions that don't cause hardness

Properties
- Dissolved Solids
- Excellent Solvent
- Expands as Freezes
- Density 1g/m³
- 1cc floats
- high bp low mp

Water Cycle
- Evaporation
- Condensation/Clouds
- Clouds Cool
- Rain
- Lakes and Rivers
- Starts Again

Electrolysis
- Elements
- Water
- $2H_2O$
- $2H_2 + O_2$
- Electricity
- Chemical Reaction

Hofmann Voltameter
- Sulphuric Acid
- Platinum Electrodes
- O_2/Anode
- H_2/Cathode

17

 # Coping with Exams

Exams are very stressful. Our body reacts to feelings of stress, so we often have physical symptoms brought on by experiencing stress.

Have you ever experienced stress?

_____

What caused this stress?

_____

_____

In groups, try role playing the situations that made you feel stressed. Tick any of the symptoms you experience or that you have experienced during stressful times:

1 Lack of appetite ☐
2 Headaches ☐
3 Tiredness ☐
4 Inability to sleep ☐
5 Butterflies in your stomach ☐
6 Feeling shaky ☐
7 Sweating ☐
8 Heart beating fast ☐
9 Passing out ☐
10 Nausea ☐
11 Irritability ☐
12 Inability to concentrate ☐
13 Tense muscles ☐

Stress can also be positive. It can help improve performance and motivate us. When you're under stress, your body releases the hormone **adrenaline** (often called the 'fight or flight' hormone), which prepares it for danger. When we are under excessive stress this hormone can cause physical symptoms that make us feel unwell. The severity of the symptoms depends on the individual. Like other types of anxiety, exam stress can create a vicious circle if it is not dealt with: the more you focus on the bad things that could happen, the more anxious you feel. This makes you feel worse and, because your head is full of negative thoughts and fears, it can increase the chance of doing badly in the exam.

Have you ever experienced any different symptoms of stress?

_____

_____

Who could you talk to if you feel stressed?

_____

_____

To minimise exam stress try the following:

1 **Study properly and be prepared**. Ensure that you know the format of the exam and how long to spend on each question. Stick to this time plan.

2 **Get enough sleep the night before the test**. Your memory recall will be much better if you've had enough rest. In a scientific study, people who got enough sleep before taking a maths test did better than those who stayed up all night studying.

3 **Listen closely to any instructions**. As the teacher hands out the test, be sure you know what's expected of you.

4 **Read through the test first**. Make sure to read it back and front. Once you have the test paper in front of you, read over the entire test, checking out how long it is and all the parts that you are expected to complete.

5 **Focus on one question at a time**. If you don't know an answer – don't panic. It's only to be expected that something will catch you out. Answer it as best you can and move on to the next question.

6 **Relax**. If you're so nervous that your mind goes blank, you might need a mini-break. Of course you can't get up and move around in the middle of a test, but you can wiggle your fingers and toes, take four or five deep breaths, or picture yourself on a beach or in some other peaceful place.

Finished early?

It's tempting to leave the exam hall. Don't. It's a good idea to spend the remaining time checking over your work. You can add details that you may not have thought you'd have time for.

Not enough time?

If you suddenly realise there is only 5 minutes left, don't panic. Use bullet points to finish the question you are doing and attempt any other questions with bullet points. Remember, you can only get marks for a question if you have attempted it.

If you do feel stressed

Try a deep breathing exercise. When you feel stressed or anxious you often forget to breathe properly. You can practise deep breathing exercises at home – playing quiet music in the background might be helpful.

Deep breathing exercise

Close your eyes.

Place your hand on your ribcage.

Take a deep breath in through your nose.

Notice that your hand moves outwards.

Imagine that your lung is divided into three sections. As you breath in, first the lower part of the lung fills with air, then the middle part (chest expands at this point) and finally the upper section of the lungs (shoulders rise upwards).

If you can, hold your breath for ten seconds and slowly breathe out. Notice that as you breathe out the tension is released and you should feel calmer. The calmest or quietest time of the breath is immediately after you've breathed out. Take note of the calmness in your body at this time.

It may feel strange to breathe in through your nose, so find a mechanism that is comfortable for you.

You should practise this technique regularly and use it when you feel anxious.

Leah

Leah is studying for her Junior Certificate. She is a bright student but lately she's found herself avoiding study. She wants to do well but finds getting started is a problem. Thinking about not studying also makes her feel stressed. Television programmes and friends calling around often distract her. If Leah has a class test she always finds herself cramming the night before and staying up late. She normally regrets not having started sooner.

Why do you think Leah finds it hard to start studying? Have you ever felt like this?

_____

_____

Putting things off can sometimes make you more stressed. What kind of things do people put off doing?

_____

_____

Write down three things that you have put off recently.

1 _____

2 _____

3 _____

List any strategies Leah could adopt to help her avoid stress. Could you apply any of these strategies to your own life?

_____

_____

Tom

Tom is a good student. He studies hard for his exams. Last week at school, the career guidance teacher told the class to start thinking about their subjects for next year. Tom has no idea what he wants to do when he leaves school and he is finding making the decision stressful.

Is there anyone Tom can talk to?

_____

What helpful advice could the group give him?

_____

Module Review

Date:

In this module I learned about: _____

I enjoyed this module because: _____

I disliked this module because: _____

I would rate this module __ out of ten for relevance to my life. This module was relevant/not relevant to my life because:

_____

_____

_____

Module 3

Communication Skills

 Learning to Communicate

In first year you explored the idea of communications and examined different ways of expressing yourself – passive, aggressive and assertive. In second year you practised expressing yourself in an assertive way. Can you remember what the characteristics of these types of communication are?

Assign each of the following mannerisms to a communication style.

Passive	Assertive	Aggressive

1 Loud voice.

2 Whining about things.

3 Using terms such as 'I guess', 'I suppose' and 'maybe'.

4 Calm, controlled voice.

5 Threatening people.

6 Direct and open.

7 Unable to accept a compliment.

8 Recognising other people's feelings.

→ Dealing with Sensitive Situations

Sometimes when communicating we have to recognise that an individual may find the issue difficult to discuss. This does not mean that one should ignore the situation.

What situations would you find difficult to discuss?

Difficult situations

Listed overleaf are a number of scenarios. Get into groups and discuss/role-play each situation. Identify the things you feel are appropriate or inappropriate.

Ruth and Jennifer have been friends for years. Last night Ruth's parents told her that Jennifer's parents have separated. Ruth feels really upset for her friend and wants to tell her how sorry she is and also let her know that if she wants to talk about it Ruth is willing to be a shoulder to cry on. She decides to talk to Jennifer.

James and Kevin have always played in midfield for their local GAA club and are great friends. Recently Kevin hasn't been playing so well and has not been selected to play for the county championship, but James has. Kevin has decided not to go and see the match and feels really angry to have been dropped. James thinks Kevin should come to the match and cheer on the team. The boys talk about the situation.

Chloe and Jake are first cousins and have always been close. Jake's mother has just been diagnosed with cancer and is undergoing chemotherapy. Jake is refusing to talk to his parents about his mother's illness and keeps telling them he is fine. Chloe knows that he is really worried about his mum and is anxious to talk with him.

During the summer holidays Mark's dad was killed in a road accident. Tom was on holiday when it happened and hasn't seen Mark since. They have always hung out together and Tom feels bad for not having made contact with Mark since his dad's death. On Saturday afternoon the two boys meet by chance in town.

Michael is going skiing with his school during the Christmas holidays. The trip is very expensive and Michael knows that his parents will find it difficult to help him pay for it. He has just found out that his dad has been made redundant and is concerned that he will have to cancel his trip. He discusses it with his dad.

If you were in each of these situations what would you do?

_____

_____

Would you normally try and avoid these situations? Why?

_____

_____

What should be said in each of these situations? What should not be said?

_____

_____

What support structures are available to you if you found yourself in a difficult situation and didn't know what to do or were upset about it?

_____

_____

Tim and Ronan have been friends since primary school. They spend a lot of time together and play basketball for their local team. Tim has noticed recently that Ronan has bad breath. At first he didn't want to say anything, but yesterday he overheard two of the girls in their class slagging Ronan off behind his back. Tim has tried offering Ronan mints and chewing gum but it hasn't worked.

Should Tim speak to Ronan about this problem?

_____

_____

How do you think Ronan will react?

_____

_____

If they are such good friends why is Tim finding it difficult to talk to Ronan about this?

_____

_____

What would you do in this situation?

_____

_____

Weekly Task

While watching a film/TV programme this week, take note of a difficult situation and observe how the characters communicate with one another. Is the situation handled well? Do any of the characters say anything inappropriate?

Communication in Situations of Conflict

In situations of conflict people often get angry. This is not always a bad thing: anger can have positive or negative effects depending on how we control it.

Positive

1 Makes us more assertive and helps us stand up for ourselves.

2 Energises us.

3 Gives us a sense of authority and self-belief.

Negative

1 Leads to aggression and temper.

2 Disrupts relationships if used too often.

Strategies for Dealing with Anger

List any other strategies you find useful.

1 Count to ten before saying anything.

2 Take several deep breaths.

3 Tell the other person you are angry and say why.

4 Listen to the other person.

5 Ask why the other person is angry.

6 Suggest solutions to the problem.

7 Walk away until you feel more composed.

8 When confronting the individual describe their behaviour, not their character.

Communication is the key to dealing with conflict.

Below are some examples of situations involving conflict. Consider what you would do in each of these situations.

Annemarie's parents allowed her to go to the local youth disco on the condition that she got home before midnight. Annemarie had arranged to come home with her friend Michelle, but Michelle didn't arrive at the meeting point until 12.10 and Annemarie doesn't get home until 12.30. Her parents are furious.

Dave and some of his friends were messing today in class before the teacher arrived — throwing paper aeroplanes, writing on the board, etc. Just as the teacher walked in Dave was throwing a ball of paper which accidentally hit the teacher. The teacher was furious and demanded to know what was going on. None of Dave's friends admitted to their role in the messing and Dave was sent to the head teacher's office. His parents have been called in and Dave knows he will be grounded and will miss his planned trip to the race track at the weekend. He meets his friends after his meeting with the head teacher.

Patrick's younger brother has borrowed his iPod without asking permission. When he returns it the screen is cracked and the earphones damaged. Patrick is raging. He had saved up for months to buy the iPod and can't believe his brother has been so careless.

Rebecca and Karen's parents have been away for the day and left a number of jobs for the girls to do. Rebecca does the washing and hangs the clothes on the line before going to town to meet her friends. When she gets home from town her parents are back and her mother is furious that the hoovering has not been done. Rebecca tries to explain but her mother doesn't want to know and sends the girls to their room. Rebecca is disgusted with Karen.

Jake's older sister borrowed money from him to buy her boyfriend a birthday present. She promised she would give it back to him by the end of the week. Three weeks have passed and Majella still hasn't returned the money. Jake needs the money to pay for his ticket to the rugby international.

Identify the main areas of conflict in your life.

_____

_____

Think of a situation when you felt very angry. What made you feel angry?

_____

_____

Did you confront someone with your anger?

_____

_____

What was the outcome of the situation?

_____

In pairs, consider the following issues for each of the situations above.

1 What is the conflict in each of these situations?

2 What caused the conflict?

3 How could it be resolved?

4 Could the conflict have been avoided?

How did you feel afterwards?

_____

_____

Was the situation resolved? How?

_____

_____

_____

Weekly Task

If you find yourself dealing with situations of conflict during the week, try to deal with your anger in a positive way by following some of the guidelines in this module.

Module Review

Date:

In this module I learned about: _____

I enjoyed this module because: _____

I disliked this module because: _____

I would rate this module __ out of ten for relevance to my life. This module was relevant/not relevant to my life because:

_____

_____

_____

Physical Health

Diet

Healthy Eating Crossword

Across
2. This food is in a hurry
3. This Italian food is a good source of carbohydrates
8. Causes narrowing of the artery walls
9. Environmentally friendly food
12. Better than fried
14. A good source of vitamin C
15. A condition caused by a lack of iron

Down
1. You do not need to be underweight to suffer from this
4. Excessive thirst is one symptom of this disorder
5. Prevents constipation
6. Energy from food is measured in _____
7. Needed to repair cells
8. Necessary for health bones and teeth
10. A healthy way to cook vegetables
11. A high-protein food from hens
13. Use this food type sparingly

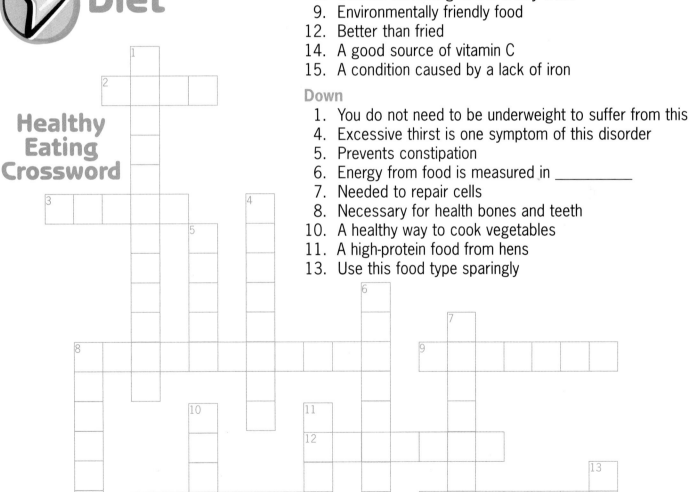

→ How Healthy Are You?

The following questionnaire will help you decide whether you have a healthy lifestyle.

1. Do you smoke?

Yes 0   No 2   Sometimes 1

2. Do you drink?

Yes 0   No 2   Sometimes 1

3. Do you eat the recommended amount of fruit and veg?

Sometimes 1   Always 2   Never 0

4. Do you use salt on your food?

Sometimes 1   Always 0   Never 2

5. How often do you eat sweets, cakes, chocolate?

Once a week 1   Every day 0   Occasionally 2

6. Do you get at least thirty minutes of physical exercise every day?

Sometimes 1   Always 2   Never 0

7. How would you describe your sleep?

Poor sleeper 0   5–6 hours a night 1   7–8 hours a night 2

8. How often do you feel under stress?

Sometimes 1   Never 2   Often 0

9. How often do you eat fried foods, chips etc?

Every day 0   Rarely 2   2–3 times a week 1

(Adapted from *Change of Heart* handbook, Health Promotion Unit)

Add up your score. The higher your score the healthier your lifestyle.

If you scored mostly 2s: well done – you are leading a healthy lifestyle.

If you scored mostly 1s: you need to improve some habits.

If you scored mostly 0s: your lifestyle is unhealthy – you need to make changes.

Can you think of one change you could make today that would improve your lifestyle?

_____

_____

 ## Ditch the Junk

Young people have more pocket money than they used to, so it is even easier to slip into bad habits, and even more important that we become responsible for our own dietary needs.

By now you're probably packing your own lunch box, so let's get active in improving eating habits. Answer the questions on the next page as honestly as you can.

How many times last week did you eat the foods listed below?

Crisps _____

Chocolate bars _____

Biscuits _____

Chips _____

Sweets _____

Ice cream_____

Dessert/whipped cream _____

Fast food _____

Cakes _____

Fried food_____

Pizza _____

You should only eat fried food, chips or crisps once or twice a week. How often did you eat these foods last week? What does this say about your diet?

_____

_____

Biscuits, desserts and chocolate should be eaten only occasionally. How many times did you eat these?

_____

How often do you snack on fatty foods during the day?

_____

Do you eat because you are bored?

_____

Do you think you eat healthily?

_____

How much would you spend on snack food per day?

_____

Food Facts

Read the information below, then fill in the blanks on page 36.

Calories

Energy produced by the body from food is measured in calories or kilojoules. Most labels refer to calories. Adolescents need 2000 to 3000 calories every day for growth. If you eat more calories than you need for the amount of physical activity you do, you will gain weight. Simply put, more calories coming in than energy going out = weight gain.

Fatty Foods

It is important to limit the amount of fat in your diet. Eating too much fat is linked to weight gain and obesity. If you eat snacks, try to choose ones that are low in fat. The recommended fat intake per day is 80 grams for teenage girls and 100–110 grams for teenage boys. The table below shows the calorific and fat content of various foods. What do you notice about the nutritional values of fast food?

Food	Fat (grams)	Calories
Big Mac	23.0	493
Medium fries	13.0	293
McChicken sandwich	17.0	375
Double Whopper with cheese	59.0	932
Bacon double cheese burger	29.0	523
Chicken curry with rice (average portion)	18.2	475
Popcorn (average portion)	4.3	135
Pringles (half a tin)	9.2	138
Packet of low-fat crisps	5.0	110
Packet of full-fat crisps	9.6	143
Danish pastry	15.0	318
Ice cream (2 scoops)	4.6	92
Apple	0.13	57
Banana	0.48	99
Potato mashed with low-fat butter (average portion)	2.0	111
Chicken fillet	5.0	163
Fresh fruit salad	0.1	77

Source: VHI Food Factfinder

Breakfast

Eating breakfast is very important. It kick starts your metabolism, helps to burn off calories and gives you energy for the morning. And it helps you concentrate in school.

Make sure to allow enough time in the morning to have breakfast. Skipping breakfast is not a good idea.

Oh, Sugar

When you eat sugary foods you might feel an immediate energy rush, but this can be followed by feeling tired and sluggish. The sugar in snack foods is absorbed straight into the bloodstream, giving an instant rush of glucose. This makes the body's blood sugar levels rise too high. The body responds to this by lowering the level of sugar in the bloodstream, which is why we can end up feeling tired. Sugary foods don't satisfy the appetite as well as other foods. (Source: Jason Vale, *Slim for Life*.)

Skipping Meals

Skipping meals is not a good idea for growing teenagers. Some people believe skipping meals can help them lose weight, but the opposite is true. What actually happens is that missing meals starves the body, which slows your metabolism, which causes fewer calories to be burned. The result is weight gain. (Source: www.sureslimuk.com.)

Fill in the Blanks

Energy produced by the body from food is measured in _____. Adolescents need between _____ and _____ calories per day for growth. If the calories taken in are greater than the calories used, this will result in weight _____. The maximum daily recommended fat intake for teenage boys is between _____ and _____ grams. Too much fat in a person's diet is linked to _____. A fast food burger could contain over _____ your daily requirement of fat. Eating a good breakfast is vital for _____ and to help teenagers _____ at school.

Too much _____ can lead to an increase in blood sugar levels, which in turn can make you feel _____. Skipping meals fools the body into thinking it is being _____, and the body in turn _____ the metabolism.

Dietary Diaries

Joan works long hours in her job. Most mornings she is in too much of a hurry to have breakfast. She eats a healthy lunch — usually a sandwich and a fruit drink. If she is home late, she might just have a bowl of cereal and some biscuits.

Do you think Joan is eating well?

_____

What long-term impact will Joan's eating habits have?

_____

What good habits does Joan have?

_____

_____

What bad habits does she have?

_____

_____

List three things she could do to improve her diet.

1 _____

2 _____

3 _____

Susan has been upset about her weight for a while now. She is very envious of some of her friends, who seem to be able to eat what they want and not put on any weight. Lately she has cut back on her food intake. She has a cup of coffee for breakfast. She does not eat lunch but finds she is starving when she gets home. Her desire to lose weight is very strong, and recently she bought some diet pills. Susan has begun to lose weight, but her friends notice she is becoming increasingly moody. She finds she gets tired more often.

Why do you think Susan is moody and tired?

_____

_____

What are the long-term effects of Susan's eating habits?

_____

_____

How can she improve her eating habits?

_____

_____

Pat usually misses breakfast because he gets up late. By his 11.00 break he is very hungry and he buys a bar of chocolate and a packet of crisps from the shop. For lunch he sometimes buys a bag of chips and a burger from the canteen. He snacks on biscuits before he has his dinner in the evening and he usually eats something before he goes to bed. Pat does not like vegetables.

List three things Pat needs to change in his diet.

1 _____

2 _____

3 _____

What could he do to replace the nutrients he does not get from vegetables?

_____

_____

What are the short-term effects of Pat's diet?

_____

Use the space below to write an account of your daily eating patterns.

Do you think you need to make any changes to your diet?

_____

_____

Write down three changes you could make now.

1 _____

2 _____

3 _____

Weekly Task

Keep a food diary for the next three days.

Try to choose healthier options and keep to the daily recommended servings of each food group.

Use the
FOOD PYRAMID
to Plan Your Healthy Food Choices

How to use the Pyramid

The recommended number of servings for children (from 5 years of age*) and adults is highlighted beside each shelf. For example, to get **at least 4 servings** from the the **Fruit and Veg** shelf you could have:

½ a glass of fruit juice= 1

3 dessertspoons of veg= 1

1 apple= 1

1 banana= 1

Total 4

choose very small amounts

Choose oils, margarine or low fat spreads labelled 'High in Polyunsaturates' or 'high in Monounsaturates' which are healthier for your heart. Use sparingly. Limit fried foods to 1-2 times a week.

choose any 2 MEAT, FISH, EGGS, BEANS & PEAS

Choose lean meats or trim off fat.
Choose 3 servings during pregnancy.

choose any 5 MILK, CHEESE & YOGURT

Choose lean meats or trim off fat.
Choose 3 servings during pregnancy.

choose any 4+ FRUIT & VEGETABLES

Choose green leafy vegetables, citrus fruit and fruit juices frequently.

choose any 6+ BREAD, CEREALS & POTATOES

Choose high fibre cereals and breads frequently.
If physical activity is high, up to 12 servings may be necessary.

DRINK WATER REGULARLY – AT LEAST 8 CUPS OF FLUID PER DAY

Folic Acid – An essential ingredient in making a baby. If there is any possibility that you could become pregnant, then you should be taking a folic acid tablet (400 micrograms a day)

* For younger children, start with smaller and fewer servings and increase up to the guidelines recommended, according to the child's own growth and appetite.

Day 1	Breakfast	
	Lunch	
	Dinner	
	Snacks	
Day 2	Breakfast	
	Lunch	
	Dinner	
	Snacks	
Day 3	Breakfast	
	Lunch	
	Dinner	
	Snacks	

 # Choose the Healthier Option

Below are some food items. Match the food type on the left-hand side with
its healthier equivalent on the right-hand side. One has been done for you.

Deep-fried chips   Fresh fruit salad

Crusty white bread roll   Brown bread sandwich

Mars bar   Cereal bar

Big Mac   Grilled burger topped with salad

Fried rice   Popcorn or low-fat crisps

Full-fat crisps   Boiled rice

Ice cream   Chicken fillet with salad

Steak and chips   Oven-baked chips

Burger and fried onions   Pasta with creamy sauce

Fast food chicken burger   Grilled steak and baked potato

Project Work

Research the link between diet and one of the diseases/health problems listed below. Present your findings to the class.

- Osteoporosis
- Cancer
- High blood pressure
- Diabetes
- Heart disease
- High cholesterol.

In your presentation, include:
1 a description of the disease/health problem (you could use pictures)
2 symptoms
3 treatments
4 links with diet.

 Nutrition and Sport

Do David Beckham, Roger Federer, Ronan O'Gara and Serena Williams approach diet differently?

In general, athletes follow a low-fat (to avoid weight gain), low-salt (to avoid dehydration), balanced diet. They have to be very tuned in to what they are eating, especially on match days and training days.

Read the following and complete the task.

Before the Game/Training

What you eat every day can have a big effect on how you perform, and what you eat just before the event or just before training is critical. The pre-game/pre-training meal can supply your body with a significant amount of energy. You should eat the right kinds of foods leading up to the event to charge your muscles with glycogen. Glycogen is a source of energy for your muscles. On the day of the game meals should be high in complex carbohydrates and low in protein. The last meal should be taken no less than three hours before the event. Breakfast could include porridge, toast and a glass of juice; another meal could be a stir fry with rice.

During the Game/Training

It is very important to get plenty of water during the game. Water stores are used up to cool the body through sweating. These water stores need to be replenished so the body can continue to cool down efficiently and the athlete does not lose concentration or become dehydrated. A commercial sports drink or a juice drink can also be considered as an alternative to water.

After the Game/Training

It's essential to refuel with carbohydrates after a game. After an event it can take an athlete 20 hours or more to replace their glycogen stores. Small amounts of protein can also aid recovery. Refuelling ideas include Weetabix, cornflakes, bananas and cereal bars.

Activity
Using the information given above, design a menu for a sports person of your choice on a game/training day.

Weekly Task

Interview a sports person you know about their diet.

 Fad Diets

The following extract highlights the dangers of fad dieting. Read the article and answer the questions that follow.

'Quick fix diets are becoming more and more common. Although weight loss is important for overweight people, these diets can produce more problems.

These diets usually restrict calorie intake or nutrients or recommend one food group over another. Examples include the cabbage diet, the three-day diet and the Atkins diet. Such fad dieting has a number of serious flaws, firstly, eliminating certain food types can result in a deficiency in nutrients. Often what appears to be weight loss is simply water loss. This type of dieting can also slow down the body's metabolic rate (the rate your body burns calories). So when you begin to eat normally again you can gain weight as your body has acclimatised itself to a certain food intake.

Banning certain food types can lead to cravings which in turn leads to binge eating and weight gain. The best way to lose weight is to eat healthily and not exclude any particular food type. Exercise and a healthy diet combined can be most effective.'

(Source: www.angelfire.com)

What are fad diets? Have you heard of any of these lately?

_____

_____

What are the dangers of fad diets?

_____

_____

What is the best way to maintain a healthy diet?

_____

_____

'As every celebrity under the sun joins the "Skinny Minnie" brigade, we are being tempted into following their regimes. But are they healthy?

'Before British model Twiggy hit the magazine stands in the mid-1960s, curvy pin-up girls such as Jayne Mansfield and Ann Margret were all the rage. But Twiggy changed that. The face of swinging '60s London had gained her nickname from her stick-thin pubescent figure.

'Although curves seemed to enjoy a renaissance in the 1980s, the waif look was predominant on the catwalk by the 1990s, with Kate Moss pioneering "heroin chic".

'These days, it isn't only models who are under pressure to remain thin. Every week another celebrity joins the "Skinny Minnie" brigade.

'The desire to emulate celebrity role models means that more and more ordinary women are resorting to increasingly drastic measures such as obsessive exercising to maintain a slim figure. "Any degree of obesity in the female population in the Western world is looked upon as ugly and undesirable," says Dr John Griffin, head of the Eating Disorder Unit at Saint Patrick's Hospital, Dublin.

'The most worrying aspect of this phenomenon is yo-yo dieting. As the stars shrink, this dangerous trend grows. In some, it can lead to an acute eating disorder.

'"There is strong evidence to show that up to 80% of people with eating disorders start out with yo-yo dieting," says Margot Brennan, public relations officer with the Irish Nutrition and Dietetic Institute. "They start out as young girls embarking on a diet and in some that becomes an obsession."

'When celebrities maintain extreme diets, the results are hardly healthy. A recent issue of *Now* magazine runs with the cover, "What Celebs Really Weigh" – demonstrating just how interested we are in this subject. Depressingly, of the 14 women featured in the article, only three are what would be considered a healthy weight for their height, namely singers Mariah Carey and Charlotte Church and model Tyra Banks. The rest, including Victoria Beckham, Liz Hurley and the emaciated Nicole Richie, fall below the weight recommended for their age and height.'

Martha Connolly,
Health Writer,
Health and Living, *Irish Independent,* 6 March 2006.

Questions for Discussion

1 Why do you think young people may want to emulate celebrities?
2 Do you agree or disagree with this article? Why?
3 Why do you think celebrities might have such a strong influence on teenagers?

Discuss the following questions in pairs.

Do you believe magazine and television ads showing images of unrealistically thin models influence teenage girls' self esteem? Explain your answer.

_____

_____

_____

Do you believe images of the ideal male body in magazines and television commercials influence males' self-esteem? Explain your answer.

_____

_____

_____

Which stereotype is portrayed more often? Do you think males or females are more influenced by media imagery?

_____

_____

_____

What changes would you make to the media's message?

_____

_____

Helpful Websites

These websites can help you explore this area further:
www.bodywhys.ie
www.healthpromotion.ie
www.irishhealth.com
www.irishheart.ie
www.mindbodysoul.gov.uk/eating
www.news.bbc.co.uk/cbbcnews
www.rte.ie
www.vhi.ie

45

Physical Exercise

Exercise Crossword

Across
6. Athletes should use this food type for energy
8. 'Happy chemicals' released during exercise
9. An exercise associated with relaxation
10. You should do at least _____ minutes of exercise three times a week to keep fit
11. It is very important to take this during exercise
13. A lack of this is often given as an excuse for not exercising

Down
1. Exercise done to music
2. An activity done during a warm-up
3. This happens to your heart rate during exercise
4. Jogging, weightlifting or gymnastics: which of these is best for cardiovascular fitness?
5. Weightlifting can improve this
7. This occurs when you over-exercise
12. As well as exercising, it's also important to have _____ periods

Activity Quiz

1. Do you take part in any physical leisure activities (e.g. walking, cycling, dancing)?
   Never ❏
   Sometimes ⭕
   Most days ☆

2. Do you walk or cycle to school?
   Never ❏
   Sometimes ⭕
   Most days ☆

3. When you exercise, do you do so:
   Lightly ❏
   Moderately ⭕
   Vigorously ☆

4. Do you take part in PE classes?
   Never ❏
   Sometimes ⭕
   Most days ☆

5. How would you describe your fitness level?
   Very unfit ❏
   Quite fit ⭕
   Very fit ☆

6. Are you physically active at home (e.g. walking the dog, hoovering,
   cleaning windows, mowing the lawn etc.)?
   Never ❏
   Sometimes ⭕
   Most days ☆

If you scored mostly ☆s: well done – keep up this level of physical activity.

If you scored mostly ⭕s: try to include more exercise in your daily routine (at least three sessions of 30 minutes' continuous exercise a week).

If you scored mostly ❏s: you need to get more active!

Do you take regular exercise? Yes _____ No _____
If you answered 'yes':

a) What type(s) of exercise do you do?

_____

_____

b) How do you feel after doing exercise?

_____

_____

If you don't exercise, why not?

_____

People exercise for many different reasons, e.g.:

fun   keep in shape
better motivation/energy   develop confidence
feel good   relieve stress
meet friends   for a healthy heart
be in a team   learn responsibility
reduce body fat   look good
better co-ordination   better flexibility
improve strength

Group these under the headings below.

Mental Benefits	Social Benefits	Physical Benefits

Which of the reasons above are most important to you?

_____

Do you think there is a connection between a healthy body and a healthy mind? Give reasons for your answer.

_____

Discuss the statement, 'People exercise to look good rather than to stay healthy.'

_____

 # Exercise Excuses

Here are some of the concerns young people may have about exercising. Maybe some of these are relevant to you. Get into groups and come up with a solution to each one. Make a poster of your ideas.

- I don't have enough time.
- I can't afford to.
- I have asthma.
- I'm too unfit.
- I don't like getting sweaty.
- I'm not very sporty.
- I hate PE.
- The weather is too bad.
- I'm embarrassed to exercise.
- I live miles away from any facilities.

It is recommended that everyone does at least thirty minutes of activity three times a week. Try to come up with some suggestions about how you could be more active at home, in school and during your leisure time. Some suggestions have been given to start you off.

At home:
Wash the car, walk to the shops

_____

_____

At school:
Cycle or walk to school, join a sports club

_____

_____

In your leisure time:
Check out local facilities

_____

_____

Weekly Task

Discuss with your PE teacher the possibility of organising an activity during lunch break to promote exercise in your school. Examples could include a skipathon, a badminton tournament, a handball tournament, or any other activity of your choice.

Ciara loved playing sports in primary school and in first year. Recently, however, she is becoming less interested. She regularly forgets her PE gear or brings a note from her mother excusing her. She finds team sports way too rough. She dreads it when the class have to go swimming.

Why do you think Ciara has lost interest in sport/exercise?

_____

Has there been an increase or a decrease in inactivity among young people? Give a reason for your answer.

_____

What would you say to Ciara to encourage her to get more exercise? List below three dangers of not exercising and three benefits of exercising.

Dangers: _____

Benefits: _____

What could Ciara do that she might find interesting and that could improve her activity levels?

_____

Do you think females have the same opportunities as males in sport?

_____

Simon loves sport, so much so that he plays hurling, football and rugby. Simon never has a problem with getting into the first team and plays with a few school teams as well as club teams. He trains nearly every day after school and some evenings to try and keep up with all the school teams and club teams.

Recently Simon has been finding it hard to concentrate in school and he often doesn't finish his homework because he is too tired in the evening. In the last rugby match he played in he made elementary mistakes, which frustrated him.

What do you think of Simon's training schedule?

_____

What do you think are the implications for Simon a) physically and b) academically if he continues to train this much?

_____

_____

What changes do you think Simon should make to improve his situation?

_____

_____

In the space provided write an account of your exercise routine.

Weekly Task

There are many 'alternative' activities teenagers can do to stay healthy and keep in shape. Some may even be available in your area. In pairs pick an alternative type of exercise and research it using the headings below. Examples could include yoga, Tae Bo, Pilates.

Activity	Description	Physical benefits	Where can you do it?

Task

Your task for the next few weeks is to organise an exercise programme. Use the following questions as a guide to help you.

1. What are your reasons for getting fit?

2. What days/times are best for you to exercise?

3. What physical activities do you most like?

4. Would you prefer to exercise alone, with a friend or with a group?

5. What could put you off doing exercise?

Task

Using your answers, create an exercise programme for the week.

Plan of Action

_____

Activities I will participate in:

_____

Days on which I will exercise:

_____

How long I will exercise for:

_____

My goals for exercising:

_____

Weekly Task

Keep a record of your progress.
For the next week keep a record of all the exercise you do. Try to keep to your plan. Remember: keep active!

	Type of exercise	Duration of exercise	How did you feel after exercising?
Monday			
Tuesday			
Wednesday			
Thursday			
Friday			
Saturday			
Sunday			

Did you achieve your goals for the week?

_____

_____

How do you feel?

_____

_____

 **Relaxation**

 **Sleep**

A good night's sleep is very important for your health and well-being. If you don't get enough sleep you'll lack energy during the day and you may find it harder to meet daily challenges. Teenagers in particular need a good night's sleep: nine and a half hours or more is recommended.

Look at the sleep diary below. This can help you keep track of your sleep patterns and relate your sleep to your energy levels.

	Time you went to bed	Time you got up	Number of hours slept	How you felt next day
Monday–Tuesday				
Tuesday–Wednesday				
Wednesday–Thursday				
Thursday–Friday				
Friday–Saturday				
Saturday–Sunday				
Sunday–Monday				

Do you think there's a relationship between the amount you slept and how you felt the next day?

_____

Was there any night when you had less than eight hours' sleep? Why? Were you watching TV, socialising, or ...?

_____

Module Review

Date:

In this module I learned about: _____

I enjoyed this module because: _____

I disliked this module because: _____

I would rate this module __ out of ten for relevance to my life. This module was relevant/not relevant to my life because:

_____

_____

_____

Module 5

Friendship

Boyfriends and Girlfriends

As you grow older you may notice that your relationships with other people change. Much of this is because as you become more mature your outlook changes. One of the relationships that may change is the male–female relationship. If your school is mixed you may notice a change in how well boys and girls in the class work together.

Have you noticed any differences?

_____

Would you prefer to be in a single-sex or mixed-sex school? What are the advantages and disadvantages of each?

_____

	Single-sex School	Mixed-sex School
Advantages		
Disadvantages		

Do young people your age socialise with the opposite sex?

_____

In what situations?

_____

How is a friendship with someone of the opposite sex different from a friendship with someone of the same sex?

_____

_____

What pressures are there on individuals to have a boyfriend/girlfriend?

_____

_____

Have you experienced these pressures?

_____

_____

_____

What is different about having a boyfriend or girlfriend and having lots of friends of the opposite sex?

_____

_____

Is there a difference between what girls and what boys expect from a boyfriend/girlfriend relationship?

What girls expect: What boys expect:

_____   _____

_____   _____

_____   _____

The most confusing thing about boys is:

_____

_____

The most confusing thing about girls is:

_____

_____

At what age are people ready to have a boyfriend/girlfriend? Explain your answer.

_____

_____

Task

You are the editor of a teenage magazine. Reply to the following letters you have received.

Dear Editor,
I have been friends with Jack since we were very young and we live beside one another. We have always spent a lot of time together and have a great laugh. Recently Jack has started behaving differently towards me when he is with the other boys from school. I have spoken to him about it but he tells me I am imagining it. I feel really cross with him. Why is he treating me this way?

Best wishes
Marian

Dear Marian,

_____

_____

Dear Editor,
I am fifteen years old and have never had a girlfriend. I have lots of female friends and fancy one of them in particular but there is just no way I could ever ask her out. The idea of it terrifies me. The rest of the lads slag me off about being a nerd but I couldn't face it if she said no. What can I do?

Yours
Glenn

Dear Glenn,

_____
_____
_____
_____
_____
_____

Dear Editor,
My friend Claire has recently started going out with a really nice guy and generally we have great fun together. However Claire doesn't want me to feel excluded and insists that I go everywhere with them but I feel really awkward and embarrassed when they hold hands and kiss. I don't want to upset Claire or stop hanging out with them. What should I do?

Yours faithfully
Julie

Dear Julie,

_____
_____
_____
_____
_____
_____
_____
_____
_____
_____
_____
_____
_____
_____
_____
_____
_____

Module Review

Date:

In this module I learned about: _____

I enjoyed this module because: _____

I disliked this module because: _____

I would rate this module ___ out of ten for relevance to my life. This module was relevant/not relevant to my life because:

_____

_____

_____

Module 6

Relationships and Sexuality

Body Image

Body image is how a person feels about his or her physical appearance. If you have a positive body image, you probably like and accept yourself the way you are. This healthy attitude allows you to explore other aspects of growing up, such as developing good friendships, growing more independent from your parents, and challenging yourself physically and mentally. Developing these parts of yourself can help boost your self-esteem.

- 'I'm fat.'
- 'I'm too skinny.'
- 'I'd love to be taller, shorter or broader.'
- 'I hate my straight hair.'
- 'I would love curly hair.'
- 'Gosh, my nose is massive.'
- 'I really would prefer a smaller nose.'
- 'I'd love to be more muscular and taller.'

Many of these statements probably sound familiar, particularly during adolescence when one's body is undergoing changes. As young people develop into teenagers, they care more about how others see them. Body image can be closely linked to self-esteem.

Do you put yourself down about your physical appearance?

If so, you're not alone. Teenagers go through lots of physical changes. And as your body changes, so does your image of yourself. Lots of people have trouble adjusting, and this can affect their self-esteem. We would all love to change something about our bodies, but what we really need to do is to change the way we see our body and how we think about ourselves.

In groups of three or four try this affirming exercise.
Write your name at the top of a page and hand it to each person in your group. On receiving a sheet each individual writes two positive statements about the person named on the sheet.

Using photographs of yourself, design a timeline showing how your physical appearance has changed since you were an infant. For each photograph identify one aspect of your appearance that you like.

 # Improving your Body Image

Perhaps you don't feel the need to improve your body image. If that's the case – well done!

If you do feel that your confidence and self-esteem would be boosted by improving your body image, the first thing to do is to recognise that your body is your own, no matter what shape or size it is.

Perhaps there are small things that you could do to make yourself more confident. If there are things about yourself that you want to change – and can change (such as how fit you are, a change of hairstyle), do this by setting realistic goals for yourself.

Can you think of any practical things you could do improve your own body image? Can you use the SMART strategy to achieve this goal? (See page 2.)

 # Advertising

It's very difficult to have a positive body image when we are constantly being bombarded by advertisements such as those on the next page. Remember: in each case the photographer probably took hundreds of pictures out of which only one was chosen; a make-up artist and hairdresser were involved; and many of the images were airbrushed or digitally enhanced.

What message do these advertisements convey?

_____

_____

Cosmetic surgery is advertised more and more frequently in newspapers and magazines. Do you think it's an appropriate method of improving self-esteem? Do you have any concerns about using surgery to boost body image?

_____

_____

Do you think cosmetic surgery such as the procedures advertised above would help improve an individual's body image?

_____

_____

Can you think of any celebrities who have undergone cosmetic surgery? Has the surgery improved how they looked? Do you think it improved their self-esteem?

_____

_____

Would you consider having cosmetic surgery? Why/Why not?

_____

_____

- Who's Gaining weight/Who's Losing Weight?
- Get the Perfect Bikini Figure in one Week
- What Celebs Really Weigh
- Lose 10lbs in 10 Days
- Get in Shape. Lose the Fat
- Get the Perfect Pecs.

Society is becoming increasingly obsessed with body image, particularly body weight. A healthy body weight has enormous benefits, but an obsession with body weight can also have negative effects on an individual's body image. Here are some headlines from newspapers and magazines.

Questions for Discussion.

1 Why do you think these statements are often found on the cover of newspapers and magazines?
2 What are the negative effects of such headlines?
3 Have a class debate on this statement:
'The media's bombardment with unrealistic images of attractiveness has a detrimental effect on many teenagers.'

Ultimately the most important thing is to be happy in oneself.

Weekly Task

Over the next week, keep a record of any headlines associated with body image in newspapers and/or magazines.

Where I am Now

Tick the statements you agree with.
Now that I am in my mid-teens:

1   I argue with my parents more often than I used to.

2   I have developed an interest in the opposite sex.

3   I am allowed make more decisions for myself.

4   I have more responsibilities at home and at school.

5   I have male and female friends whom I confide in.

6   My parents expect me to look after my younger brothers and sisters.

7   I am allowed have a summer job and earn my own money.

8   I feel more feminine/masculine than I used to.

9   My body shape has changed.

10 My school work has become more challenging and the teachers expect us to do more work at home.

11 I have opinions of my own on political and social issues.

12 I have a mobile phone and feel more independent.

13 I buy my own clothes without consulting my parents.

14 My friends play an increasingly important role in my life.

15 I am more interested in how I look.

16 I spend time on my appearance and am conscious of changes in fashion.

17 I have developed an interest in a style of music.

18 I have a later curfew than I used to have.

Lorcan and Cian are in third year. For the past year Cian has worked on Saturdays in his parents' shop and has got paid for it. Whenever Lorcan goes out with friends or into town he has to ask his parents for money. He finds this really frustrating and now he wants to get a weekend job like Cian. His parents are adamant that he should not get a job and should focus on his studies. They have a huge row and Lorcan storms out of the house.

Why do you think Lorcan finds it annoying to have to ask his parents for money?

_____

_____

Is his frustration understandable?

_____

_____

Why do you think his parents don't want him to get a part-time job? Are their feelings justified?

_____

_____

What aspects of this situation highlight the difficulties of adolescence?

_____

_____

What could Lorcan and his parents do to sort out their disagreements so that both parties feel satisfied with the outcome?

_____

_____

Relationships – What's Important?

List the significant relationships in your life at the moment. Which are the most important to you?

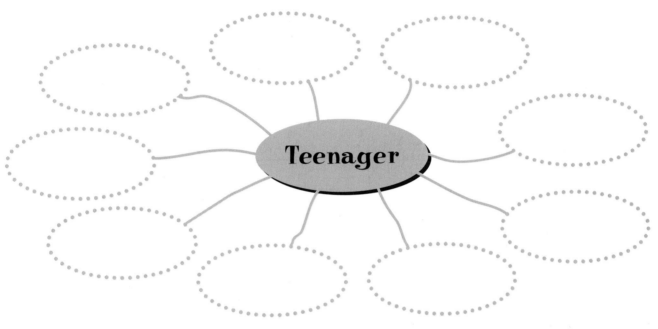

Imagine yourself in fifteen years' time. Can you predict what the significant relationships will be in your life then? Highlight the relationships you expect to be most important to you.

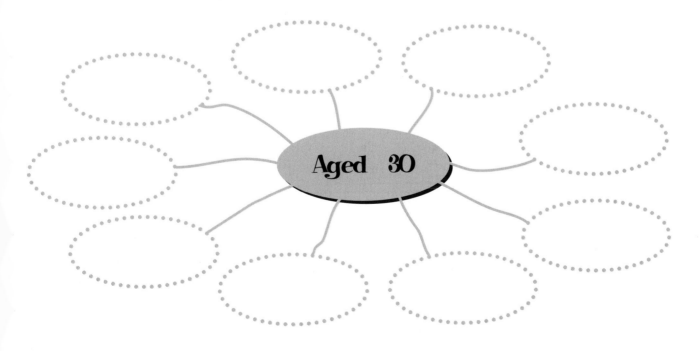

Are the relationships you expect to be important in fifteen years' time the same as the important ones now?

_____

_____

Why might the relationships that are important to you now be less important – or not important at all – in later life?

_____

_____

What types of behaviour might cause a relationship to break down?

_____

_____

Now focus specifically on a long-term relationship you imagine might exist in your life in fifteen years.

Answer the following questions about the relationship you imagine you might have then; or discuss this with a partner.

What age will you be when you meet this person? _____

Are you the same age? Is this important? _____

How will you meet, do you imagine? _____

_____

How will you get to know one another? _____

_____

How will you know that this is the right person for you? Will it be love at first sight? _____

_____

What qualities will your partner have that makes them attractive to you?

_____

What interests will you share? _____

_____

How will your relationship affect relationships with friends, parents, brothers and sisters? _____

_____

Will you get married? If so, why would you decide to get married?

_____

_____

How long will you know the person before you get married (if you do decide to get married)? _____

_____

Will you have similar religious beliefs? Is this important?

_____

_____

Will you decide to have children? If yes, how many?

_____

How will having children affect your relationship with one another?

_____

_____

At what age will you have your first child? Why this age?

_____

_____

How will the children be cared for? Who will look after them during the day? Who will be responsible for them when they wake at night? Who will go to parent–teacher meetings, bring them to sporting events etc.?

_____

_____

Would you be willing to change your work situation to look after the children? How might this affect your relationship with your partner?

_____

_____

Weekly Task

Discuss with a parent/guardian, or another adult with whom you have a good relationship, how they met their partners and what attracted them to each other.

The Three Rs – Respect, Rights and Responsibilities

All healthy relationships are based on mutual respect.

List some of the ways we show respect to those around us.

Being in any relationship means that those involved have both rights and responsibilities. Outline the rights one has in the relationships shown in the table:

Relationship	Rights and Responsibilities	
Teacher–Pupil	Teacher	Pupil
Husband–Wife	Husband	Wife
Friends		
Doctor–Patient	Doctor	Patient
Boyfriend–Girlfriend	Boyfriend	Girlfriend
Parent–Daughter/Son	Parent	Daughter/Son
Retailer–Consumer	Retailer	Consumer
Employer–Employee	Employer	Employee
Other		

➡ Role Plays

With a partner, role-play the following situations in a way that allows both parties to demonstrate the three Rs – respect, rights and responsibilities.

Or, on your own, identify the rights and responsibilities of each party and suggest a way of resolving the issue that demonstrates mutual respect.

Mark and Joanna have been going out for a year. Joanna is crazy about Mark but doesn't like the way he behaves around some of the other girls. It makes her feel awkward and jealous and she questions whether Mark is faithful. She asks him not to spend time with them, especially when she is not with him.

Mairead has kept a diary since she was a young girl. She used to share some of the entries with her mother but in recent years has stopped doing this. Many of the things she writes are personal about herself and her friends and she would be embarrassed if anyone were to read them. She walked into her room yesterday and found her mother holding her diary. She was devastated to think her mother read her diary. A massive row followed.

Paul and Diane have been married for ten years and they have three young children. When they had their first child they decided that Diane would give up work and look after the kids until they started school. That was almost six years ago and although their youngest is only two Diane feels quite isolated and desperately wants to go back to work. Paul isn't in favour of her going to work until all the children start primary school. They discuss the problem.

Ciara and Shane have been going out for six months. They get on well but recently Ciara has started drinking when they are with friends. She frequently gets really drunk and makes a fool of herself. Shane doesn't approve and really hates the way she tells other people private things about their relationship. He sometimes drinks himself but not to the same extent as Ciara. He decides to confront her.

Weekly Task

Make a note of any time during the week you feel your rights have been ignored.

Module Review

Date:

In this module I learned about: _____

I enjoyed this module because: _____

I disliked this module because: _____

I would rate this module __ out of ten for relevance to my life. This module was relevant/not relevant to my life because:

_____

_____

_____

Stress

Stress is caused by pressure in our lives. Stress can have different meanings for different people. It can be positive when it motivates us to get things done but negative when we feel permanently pressured by constant demands. People need a certain degree of stress in order to reach targets. Too little stress can make people unmotivated and sometimes leads them to avoid confrontation.

Tick which phrases below best describe you. Discuss the negative and positive implication of each in your life.

- I am calm and unhurried about appointments.
- I like things I do to be perfect.
- I can't accept delays.
- I rarely hurry even when pressurised.
- I often repeat old arguments in my head.
- I usually avoid confrontation even if I feel wronged.
- I am very competitive.
- I am not at all competitive.
- I avoid doing things because I'm afraid I might fail.
- I love a challenge.
- I often let others set my deadlines.
- I don't mind leaving things unfinished.
- I must complete a task.
- I take school very seriously and have few outside interests.

Positive	Negative

Write about a time you experienced positive stress.
Write about a time you experienced negative stress.

 # Symptoms of Stress

Stress can be mental (affecting your mind) or physical (affecting your body).
Group the following symptoms of stress into physical and mental symptoms.

lack of concentration   dizziness   headaches

frustration   sweating   AGGRESSION

tiredness   lack of interest   breathing faster

nausea   excessive smoking or drinking

sleep problems   depression

nail biting   feelings of being a failure

forgetfulness   over-eating or loss of appetite

Physical Symptoms	Mental Symptoms

Task

Get together in groups and come up with a list of some of the demands placed on teenagers under each of the following headings.

- Family
- Friends
- School
- Boyfriend/girlfriend
- Appearance.

 Teenage Stress

Listed below are some sources of teenage stress. In groups, discuss what steps you could take if you had one of these problems. For example, who could you talk to? (Teacher, school counsellor, help lines, agencies, etc.)

- School demands
- Negative self-image
- Physical changes
- Problems with friends
- Unstable/unsafe home life
- Parents separating/divorcing
- Teenage pregnancy
- Illness in the family
- Death of a loved one
- Family financial problems
- Moving to a different area
- Family member taking drugs
- Taking on too much
- Bullying
- In trouble with the law
- Breaking up with a boyfriend or girlfriend
- Putting things off.

Responses to Stress

We are often unprepared for stressful situations. The way people respond to stress can vary. Tick the boxes below that come closest to your own responses to stress.

Worry excessively. . . . . ❏
Cry . . . . ❏
Ignore it and hope it will go away . . . . ❏
Walk away . . . . ❏
Try to sort it out on your own . . . . ❏
Pretend nothing is wrong . . . . ❏
Get angry/lose your temper . . . . ❏
Discuss it with a friend or family member. . . . . ❏
Laugh it off/make a joke of it . . . . ❏
Become quiet and avoid people. . . . . ❏
Keep busy, try to keep your mind off it . . . . ❏
Play a match/go for a run. ❏
Blame yourself . . . . ❏
Forget about – it's over. . . . . ❏
Take time out and go to a place you like . . . . ❏
Have negative thoughts, e.g. 'I'll never pass the exam' . . . . . ❏

 # Individual Work

Do you think your coping styles are effective in relieving your stress? Why/why not?

_____

_____

Sometimes people are reluctant to share their problems. Why do you think this is?

_____

_____

79

What are the benefits of confiding in someone about a problem?

_____

_____

Below are some positive stress busters. Discuss the benefits of each.

- Use humour
- Relax and treat yourself
- Exercise
- Accept what you cannot change
- Eat a good diet
- Take one thing at a time
- Make lists
- Talk to someone
- Take up a hobby

Discuss the following questions in pairs.

1 Do you think males and females differ in the way they cope with stress? In what way?
2 Is there more pressure on males than females to cope with their own problems?
3 Do you think it is easier for males or females to show how they feel?
4 Do you think boys are discouraged from showing their feelings?
5 Do you believe there are feelings girls are discouraged from showing?

It's do or diet for our teens

It's no picnic being a teenage girl if the results of a new survey are anything to go by. Girls as young as 13 claim dieting has become a norm among their peers and topics of conversation revolve around calories and carbs, fitness and fat.

'Such is the strain that a recent survey in the United Kingdom reveals that one in ten describes themselves as an emotional wreck. The survey of 2000 teenagers carried out by Bliss magazines cited forty per cent of those surveyed saying they regularly feel depressed.

'And it would seem that Irish teens have similar troubles to contend with. The Celtic Tiger may have brought greater choice and financial ease to a new generation, but there is a darker side to our economy boom. Family problems, academic pressures, bullying in school, and a societal obsession with the "flawless figure" are identified by teenage girls as the key stresses in modern Ireland.

'Emma Grimes (17) is an active and intelligent young woman but she says she would not dream of going to school without wearing make-up. There are thousands of girls out there like her who won't leave their bedroom until they have applied that all-important barrier between them and a very cruel world. "Without a doubt girls my age worry about their image, I know a lot of girls who suffer from bulimia and anorexia and they were never fat."

'She feels that the media is partly to blame for the modern obsession of adopting extreme measures to achieve the perfect body, sentiments echoed by her sister Orla (13). "TV programmes like *The Swan* make it seem like if you're not perfect, no one will like you."

'Whilst Orla feels that the young teenagers don't judge each other as much on their looks, Emma says that the obsession with image is affecting people at a younger age every day. "Most first years in my school wear foundation every day, we didn't at that age." Emma maintains that life doesn't get easier as you get older. "You don't just have your own problems, you have your friends' problems too and you do worry about these."

'She admits sometimes feeling low as a result of these issues and believes the time has come to introduce more "coping with life" topics into the curriculum. Bullying by their peers further increases the stresses facing teenage girls.

'Lucia McGranaghan (17), from Strabane, Co Tyrone, says one of the quickest ways to get you down is for someone to make a negative comment about your appearance. "Girls can be bitchy. Some people may accept you for who you are, but for others you have to look a certain way and it's generally in terms of weight."

'The insensitivity of their male peers strongly contributes to the hurt of having a poor self image. "Guys always go on about thin celebrities. They are really critical and these are often guys who are nothing to look at themselves." In one Dublin school, teenage boys actually run their own version of Miss World, they vote on which of the girls has the best body. And this is around 16 years of age!

'"People do worry about weight when someone makes a comment and many go on diets even when they don't need to."

Pressure

'Lucia is taking her A levels this year and says exam pressures can really get you down. "Everyone is worried now. There are days when people can be really down about it." Still, she feels that exam pressures are a normal part of getting on in life and, in an isolated context, can be dealt with. "It's only if they are added to pressure from people your own age about how you look that people will really feel depressed." Jill Cousins (17), from Castleknock, is doing her Leaving Cert this year and says students are getting more worried: "Some girls were actually crying after the mock exams."

'Like Lucia, however, Jill sees exam pressures as only a contributory factor to the problems. "Figure is the number one concern. Topics of conversation are always about dieting."

Dublin-based counselling psychologist Lakshmy Gunawardhana believes that proper communication is the key to putting such pressures into perspective. "Silence is a big thing. Young people don't talk enough. Talk to everyone: family, friends, neighbours. Once you start talking to people they will find their voices, then they'll be able to talk to their children."

Evening Herald,
Tuesday 8 March 2005.

Questions for Discussion

1 Do you agree with the opinions of the teenagers in this article?

2 Have you ever experienced any of the sentiments expressed by people in this article? In what circumstances?

3 Do you believe the views in this article are representative of a small minority or the majority of teenagers?

4 Do you think the girls are being fair to the male population?

5 This article suggests that the media and society put more pressure on young girls than on young boys. Do you think this is accurate? Do you believe males experience similar pressures?

6 If you could rewrite the message sent out by the media to teenagers, what would it be?

Weekly Task

Collect articles from magazines and newspapers that you feel give positive and negative messages to teenagers. Make a poster from a collage of the pictures.

The Media and Teenage Pressure

In groups, discuss the influence of the media on teenagers under the headings listed below.

- Newspaper articles that quote statistics on teenage sexuality.
- Newspaper pictures containing images of teenagers.
- Television soap operas' portrayal of teenage behaviour and issues.
- Magazine articles and the messages they convey to teenagers about what is 'normal', 'desirable', 'cool'.
- Popular music lyrics and the world view they present to and about teenagers.
- Films aimed at teenagers and what they suggest to teenagers about themselves and their lives.
- What you will never find in the media about being a teenager.

Write a Letter

You are unhappy with a programme you watched on television lately. You feel its portrayal of what is 'normal' and 'cool' behaviour for teenagers is placing pressure on teenagers to look and behave in a certain way. Write a letter outlining your dissatisfaction.

Biased adults 'stereotype, mistreat and demean young'

Teenagers hit out at treatment by teachers, gardai and politicians

By Kathy Donaghy

'Threatening, loud, noisy, troublesome and given to excess. This is the way young Irish people feel they are being stereotyped by the adults with whom they come in contact.

'A new report – 'Inequality and the Stereotyping of Young People' – to be published today by the Equality Authority and the National Youth Council of Ireland sets out a remarkable and disturbing consensus among young people as to how they are stereotyped and mistreated by adults.

'They consistently speak of being treated in a demeaning way by the education system, in shops and public places, by the gardai, by politicians, by the media and by adults in their own communities.

'In 90 interviews conducted by Dr Maurice Devlin of NUI Maynooth, young people shared a consensus that their treatment by adults was unfair.

'They told how they were followed by security guards in shops just because they were teenagers and of gardai "hassling" them. They also spoke of negative media stereotypes, where the newspapers "never had any of the good stuff we do" reported. "It's all trouble, vandalism, joyriding, drinking, drugs and smoking," one young interviewee said.

'They also held the view that while there were positive images, these were more limited in scope, featuring "youngsters in football, on the back pages" or "big swots from Blackrock or somewhere".

'The interviewees spoke of the tensions associated with hanging around and being moved on. This was linked to the lack of things to do, or at least little that was attractive or accessible.

Expecting

'"Everybody stares at you, there's nowhere to go like. As adults, they can go to the pub, they've more things to do with their time. We haven't," one interviewee, Eamon, stated.

'Another, Carmel, said: "Everybody's expecting you to cause trouble. They're looking out their windows to see what you're doing. They just expect the worse from us."

'Karen said: "All of us get tarred with the same brush. You're a teenager, you hang around in a group, you must be a vandal."

'On their relations with the gardai, interviewees said that while there were very good community gardai, many gave examples of "run-ins" with gardai, or of "not being taken seriously" or treated in a demeaning manner. Sarah pointed out that some guards "got out of the car with an attitude".

'Equality Authority chief executive Niall Crowley said the report broke important new ground in our search for a more equal society.

'"It gives a voice to young people in setting out their views on how they are perceived by adults," he said. "The discussions recorded in the focus groups pose particular challenges to journalists, politicians, the gardai, security personnel and teachers."

'Mr Crowley said it would be important to respond positively to the report. "The report exposes a stereotyping of young people that alienates, diminishes and excludes young people. It highlights a disrespect for them and a failure to accord attention to their views."

'The report recommends that factors which create or exacerbate tensions in relationships between adults and young people at neighbourhood level be addressed. These include a lack of places and spaces, both indoor and outdoor, for young people to "hang out" in a manner not considered problematic. It says there is a need for those working with young people to be aware of the effects of negative stereotyping.'

Irish Independent, Wednesday 22 February 2006

Questions for Discussion

1 Do you agree or disagree with this article?
2 Why do you think the media and adults think as they do?
3 What do you think is meant by the statement 'tarred with the same brush'?
4 What do you think are the implications of this for teenagers?

The following are examples of stressful situations for young teenagers. Read through them and then answer the questions or use the questions as a starting point for a discussion.

Joanne is best friends with Caroline. Caroline has recently become very interested in boys. At the moment she is seeing Paul. Caroline finds it easy to talk to lads, but Joanne is very shy around them. Caroline keeps pressurising Joanne to kiss Paul's friend Niall. Joanne is nervous and doesn't want to meet up with him, but she's too embarrassed to tell Caroline because she feels Caroline won't understand. Now she thinks she'll just go along with it so as not to look stupid.

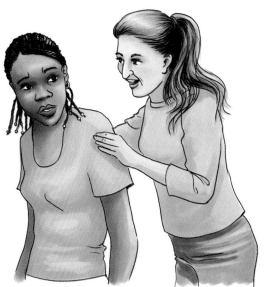

How do you think Joanne is feeling? Why is she embarrassed to tell her friend?

_____

_____

What should she do?

_____

_____

Keith's parents are constantly arguing. Just last night he was kept awake by their rowing. Keith wishes his parents would stop arguing and he's afraid they are going to separate. Lately he's been finding it difficult to concentrate in school because his mind keeps wandering back to his worries. He feels teachers just give him a hard time and they don't understand. Sometimes he feels he is to blame for his parents' arguments. Keith feels he can't tell his mates about his home troubles — they never talk about things like that. Lately he's been feeling very down, and instead of his problems going away they keep getting worse.

How is Keith's home life affecting him?

_____

_____

Do you think he is right not to talk to his friends?

_____

_____

What could Keith do to help the situation?

_____

_____

Feelings and Moods

Adolescents experience lots of different feelings, moods and emotions.
Role-play the following scenarios.

Connor wants to go out on Saturday night with his friends to a nightclub in the city centre. His parents have told him he can go to a teenage disco but he is not allowed go to a place where alcohol is being served. Connor reacts very badly to this. He tells his parents they are really unfair and that he wishes he had normal parents like everyone else.

Lauren is watching her favourite television programme. Her mother asks her to go to the shop for her. Lauren refuses to go, saying she is always asked to do everything.

Questions for Discussion

1 What do you think are the consequences of reacting in this way?
2 How could they have reacted differently?
3 Think of a recent situation in which you reacted badly. How did you feel afterwards? What would you have done differently?

Feelings

```
E  J  Z  D  Y  V  K  R  Q  R  E  S  M  D  F
R  M  A  S  L  P  G  A  E  Z  R  Y  E  Y  Z
D  S  B  X  C  U  P  S  Z  Z  E  M  D  R  Z
B  E  Z  A  I  A  P  A  Z  B  A  P  F  G  U
G  R  T  L  R  E  R  M  H  H  Q  A  T  N  S
S  B  T  I  C  R  Z  E  S  R  J  T  M  A  U
T  Y  F  T  C  P  A  A  D  X  H  H  X  R  O
U  N  E  S  T  X  Y  S  K  G  W  E  M  J  I
P  D  E  D  A  B  E  E  S  U  A  T  K  P  V
I  Y  L  E  N  O  L  P  P  E  X  I  N  W  N
D  C  S  U  O  V  R  E  N  S  D  C  H  A  E
F  U  R  I  O  U  S  P  R  J  F  W  M  I  K
M  B  J  G  I  J  J  V  D  Q  S  P  V  Y  T
U  R  I  B  Y  E  D  X  N  A  A  B  T  O  W
M  W  G  Y  V  I  R  P  R  R  H  X  I  G  E
```

ANGRY	ASHAMED	EMBARRASSED
ENVIOUS	EXCITED	FURIOUS
GUILTY	HAPPY	LONELY
NERVOUS	RESPECTED	SAD
SCARED	STUPID	SYMPATHETIC

Find the feelings in the wordsearch, then place them in the appropriate columns below.

Positive Feelings	Negative Feelings

→ **This is how I Feel**

Complete these sentences.

I am good at _____

I hope that _____

I feel sad when _____

I am most happy when _____

I feel angry when _____

I regret that _____

I believe that _____

I am proud of_____

Change is a necessary part of living. So is loss. We have all experienced changes in our lives that resulted in loss. Look at the list and circle any changes that have been part of your life. Add any other significant changes you have experienced.

- new brother or sister
- lost a friend
- grandparent died
- parents separated
- parent died
- moved house
- pet died
- changed school
- parent became unemployed
- was hospitalised
- moved country.

Everyone copes with loss in his or her own unique way, and individuals will experience different emotions.

Tick the feelings you have experienced at times of loss.

Angry ❏	Lonely ❏	Confused ❏
Shocked ❏	Tired ❏	Loved ❏
Sad ❏	Afraid ❏	Disbelieving ❏
Numb ❏	Anxious ❏	Hurt ❏
Hopeless ❏	Guilty ❏	Accepting ❏
Tearful ❏	Needed ❏	Rejected ❏
Cheated ❏	Relieved ❏	Exhausted ❏
Empty ❏	Unprepared ❏	Scared ❏
Worried ❏		

Other: _____

Were your emotions different each time you suffered a loss?

_____

_____

How did you deal with your loss?

_____

_____

Was there anything you found helpful in coping with your loss?

_____

_____

Was there anything you did not find helpful?

_____

_____

_____

Here are some of the ways you can help someone who has experienced a loss.

Do:

- Say you're sorry about what happened.
- Offer a hug.
- Let them talk about their loss as much and as often as they want.
- Keep in touch.
- Write a letter or a card.
- Call to their house.
- Find small ways to show you care.
- Allow yourself to cry if that's what you feel like.
- Accept their tears.

Don't:

- Avoid them because you feel awkward.
- Say 'I know how you feel.' (You don't.)
- Tell them they should be thankful for ...
- Avoid talking to them.
- Tell them how they should be feeling or what they should be doing.
- Exclude them from any get-togethers or events.
- Encourage them to use alcohol as a means of escaping.

Weekly Task: Worry box

During the week you might come up against something that upsets or troubles you.

Answer the questions below on a separate page. When you have finished put the sheet away in a worry box and do not think about it again until you have set a time to return to the worry box. You will find when you go to the worry box again your previous worry will be sorted out.

Solve That Problem

1 Think of a problem that has been worrying you. Explain it.

2 Think of all the thoughts you are having about this problem. Describe them.

3 How could you change these thoughts from negative to positive?

4 What advice would you give to a friend with a similar problem?

(Source: Health Promotion Unit, *Managing Stress for a Healthy Heart*)

Helpful Websites

www.channel4.com/health
www:faceup.ie
www.healthpromotion.ie
www.irishhealth.com
www.irishheart.ie
www.mindbodysoul.gov.uk/emotional
www.news.bbc.co.uk/cbbcnews
www.rte.ie
www.topics4living.com/stress_test.htm
www.vhi.ie

Module Review

Date:

In this module I learned about: _____

I enjoyed this module because: _____

I disliked this module because: _____

I would rate this module __ out of ten for relevance to my life. This module was relevant/not relevant to my life because:

_____

_____

_____

Module 8

Influences and Decisions

 ## Making Good Decisions

The people we meet during our lives have an impact on our attitudes and behaviour. Sometimes we recognise people as being good role models and we bring their attitudes and beliefs to our own lives. We all know people we look up to and admire.

Write down the name(s) of some well-known people whom you admire.

_____

_____

Choose one of the people and give three reasons why you admire him or her.

1 _____

2 _____

3 _____

Think about your own life for a moment and consider all the people who have influenced you in both positive and negative ways. Select someone from this group whom you admire. Why do you admire them?

_____

_____

What qualities do you admire in this person?

_____

_____

Can you think of a specific incident or event that highlights this individual's admirable qualities?

_____

_____

How could you incorporate this person's admirable qualities into your own life?

_____

_____

Task

Decisions

Who are the biggest influences in your life at the moment?

Using pictures, photographs, old magazines, etc., make a collage representing the current influences in your life. Are there people in your collage you do not know personally? Do these people influence your life in the same way as those you spend time with?

In what way do these people influence your attitudes, behaviour, lifestyle and friendships? In the table overleaf write in the names of the people who influence your life and identify the way they affect it.

	Name			
How they influence you:				
What you wear to school				
What you eat for school lunch				
What you wear at weekends				
Music you listen to				
TV you watch				
Activities you take part in				
People you are friends with				
Language you use				
Clubs you belong to				

Do you think that the people who influence your life at the moment will still influence your life in 15 years' time?

_____

_____

What differences would you expect to see if you completed this task when you are in your thirties?

_____

_____

Are there individuals who you feel will have a lasting effect on your life?

_____

_____

Situations

Read the following situations and discuss what should or could be done in each. Also think about what you might do if you were in a similar situation.

Aoife is in town with a group of friends on Saturday afternoon and they are all having a great time, just chatting and hanging out. One of her friends suggest going to a cafe in a nearby town to meet up with more friends. The girls have no way of getting there and they suggest hitching a lift. Aoife's parents have warned her never to do this. Her friends encourage her, saying that nothing will happen them if they stay together. She does not know what to do.

Who/what will influence her decision?

_____

_____

_____

What would you do if you were in her situation?

_____

_____

_____

What are the risks involved in Aoife's decision?

_____

_____

_____

It's James's birthday and his friend Gary has been allowed to stay over. They have also been allowed to go to the local disco, on condition that they get home by 12.30. At the end of the night Gary is reluctant to leave as he has met up with his girlfriend Deirdre and her friends. He pleads with James to stay on, saying that his curfew is usually later and anyway James's parents won't give out to him in front of his best friend. James is having too much fun and doesn't want to leave but he knows his parents will be waiting up for them and will probably be furious.

What are James's thoughts, do you imagine?

_____

_____

Do you think his parents will be worried about him? Why?

_____

_____

_____

Is it fair that Gary should abide by the curfew James's parents have set?

_____

_____

_____

What should James do?

_____

_____

Donal, Sean and David were chatting at break one day about the things their parents allow them to do. Donal and Sean were grumbling about their parents, saying how dull and boring they were. David felt he had to join in and began slagging off his Mum and Dad too. Later on he felt guilty about it. His parents work really hard and even though money is scarce they always manage to cater for David and his brothers. He gets on really well with both his parents and spends a lot of time with his Dad in particular.

Have you ever been in this or a similar situation?

_____

_____

_____

Is there anything David could do to put things right and make him feel better?

_____

_____

_____

How do you know when you have made a good decision?

_____

_____

_____

How do you know when you have made a bad decision?

_____

_____

_____

Sometimes when we make a simple decision we don't realise that it can have a long-term effect on our lives.

What long-term consequences might the following actions have?

Smoking cannabis: _____

_____

_____

Hitch-hiking: _____

_____

_____

Taking a CD from the local music store: _____

_____

_____

Walking home alone: _____

_____

_____

Getting into a fight outside a disco: _____

_____

_____

Drinking alcohol: _____

_____

_____

Having unprotected sex: _____

_____

_____

Making an uninformed subject choice for Leaving Cert: _____

_____

What decisions have you made that will have long-term effects on your life? Did you make the right decision? Who helped you make this decision?

_____

_____

_____

Where could you go to get help to make the decisions about the situations listed above? Discuss this in groups of three or four.

Module Review

Date:

In this module I learned about: _____

I enjoyed this module because: _____

I disliked this module because: _____

I would rate this module ___ out of ten for relevance to my life. This module was relevant/not relevant to my life because:

_____

_____

_____

Module 9

Substance Use

Reasons for Drug Use

B	C	H	N	J	B	L	I	K	Y
O	S	U	O	I	R	U	C	H	E
R	I	Y	I	T	U	E	Q	T	P
E	S	S	L	P	Z	S	A	L	Z
D	Y	S	L	M	D	C	E	A	C
O	G	Z	E	I	M	A	G	E	Q
M	A	V	B	R	S	P	R	H	S
K	X	T	E	U	T	I	V	F	D
Q	E	E	R	U	S	S	E	R	P
N	T	E	P	G	M	M	P	G	Y

BOREDOM

HEALTH

PRESSURE

CURIOUS

IMAGE

REBELLION

ESCAPISM

PLEASURE

STRESS

 # Ecstasy: The Realities

 ## What is it?

Ecstasy is a drug that was developed in the 1990s and is associated with raves and discos. It's a hallucinogenic amphetamine, sold in tablet form, with the chemical name MDMA. It has various street names, including 'Edward', 'E', 'Essence', 'Love Doves', 'Denis the Menace' and 'Disco Biscuits'.

The Effects of Ecstasy

1 Ecstasy begins to have an effect within an hour. The effects last from three to six hours.

2 Symptoms include feelings of relaxation, increased energy and happiness. Users may experience feelings of calmness and may feel less inhibited.

3 Users often want to dance for hours and there is a risk of overheating and dehydration if the fluid lost is not replaced.

 # The Risks

1 Users experience intense sweating, dry mouth, loss of appetite and an increase in heart rate and blood pressure.

2 They may also get pain and stiffness in the joints.

3 Users suffering from epilepsy, diabetes, asthma or heart disease become particularly vulnerable if they take ecstasy.

4 Injuries can be caused by reaction to the drug.

5 It can leave users feeling depressed and paranoid for days.

6 Many of these symptoms can result in death.

Long-term Effects

Research is still being carried out into the long-term effects of ecstasy, but we do know they include:

Most ecstasy tablets are mixed with other drugs that can be dangerous in themselves.
(Source: *Health Promotion Unit Understanding Drugs*)

1   insomnia

2   weight loss and anorexia

3   depression

4   panic attacks

5   liver damage

6   psychological dependence

7   nerve damage.

What is the chemical name for ecstasy? _____

Why do people take ecstasy? _____

_____

How long does it take ecstasy to start having an effect and how long do the symptoms last?

_____

_____

List three short-term effects of taking ecstasy.

1 _____

2 _____

3 _____

Why are people with heart disease, epilepsy and asthma particularly vulnerable? _____

_____

List three possible long-term effects of using ecstasy.

1 _____

2 _____

3 _____

Ecstasy

```
G  I  H  P  D  D  A  N  C  I  N  G
G  S  F  Y  T  E  L  B  A  T  A  X
V  Z  E  R  X  H  H  M  G  M  N  P
D  G  P  V  M  Y  C  N  V  S  X  U
M  B  X  R  A  D  I  V  I  S  I  G
S  O  D  E  P  R  E  S  S  I  O  N
X  U  S  W  E  A  T  I  N  G  U  I
I  I  W  V  L  T  Z  B  D  Q  S  B
Y  D  I  Z  Z  I  N  E  S  S  T  B
N  H  F  D  I  O  N  A  R  A  P  U
S  R  E  G  A  N  E  E  T  Z  E  L
N  K  Y  A  D  E  S  U  F  N  O  C
```

ANXIOUS	CLUBBING	CONFUSED
DANCING	DEHYDRATION	DEPRESSION
DIZZINESS	PARANOID	RAVES
SHIVERING	SWEATING	TABLET
TEENAGERS		

The Night Out

Jane and Louise have been best friends for years. They loved their Saturday nights: getting dressed up, going out and reliving the funny and memorable events of their night out the following day. Jane and Louise always used to say to each other, 'You're only young once', and the more fun they had the better. On a night out a few months ago Jane and Louise decided to take an ecstasy tablet. Jane did not particularly like the experience, but Louise continued to take ecstasy on their nights out. Jane does not much enjoy going out with Louise any more: she doesn't like the company Louise keeps, and now Louise has started to experiment with other drugs. Jane is very concerned about her friend as she is really starting to change. Jane has heard bad stories about ecstasy and is concerned for Louise. She wants to help her but she does not know who she can confide in.

Who could Jane talk to to help her friend?

_____

_____

_____

Why do you think Jane is afraid to tell someone?

_____

_____

_____

What might happen if she says nothing?

_____

_____

_____

What do you think the girls meant by 'You're only young once'? What are the dangers of thinking like this?

_____

_____

Sarah's death should be a warning to others

A mother's heartache

'Joan Murphy shows me the picture of her beautiful daughter on her sixteenth birthday. By all accounts she was a bright, lively and well-liked young girl. Joan tells me she had so much to look forward to and now it's all gone. And why? Joan tells her story.

'"Sarah had been looking forward to her night out all week. At first I was reluctant to let her go, but she was a sensible girl and she promised me that I had nothing to worry about." The sixteen year old got ready early. "She said goodbye to me and went to meet friends in town. That was the last time I saw her alive."

'Sarah had gone with friends to a disco in the city centre. She had consumed quite a bit of alcohol and then she and her friends took ecstasy. Sarah's friends had regularly taken ecstasy but Sarah had always resisted. This time she decided to give it a go.

'Sarah collapsed three hours after taking the pill. A friend found her in the bathroom. She was rushed to hospital but was pronounced dead on arrival. "If you could have seen my beautiful daughter who died taking this drug it all seems so pointless."

'A post mortem revealed that Sarah died from swelling of the brain, which occurred due to drinking too much water.

'"My family life has been devastated and I cannot stress enough the dangers of taking this drug. Sarah was a great daughter and friend. I will never understand why she took the tablet that night. If she knew the heartbreak she left behind I'm sure she would never have done it."'

How do you feel when you read stories like this?

_____

_____

_____

Do you think shock stories like this would deter young people from taking drugs?

_____

List two risks associated with taking ecstasy.

1 _____

2 _____

Why do you think Sarah took ecstasy?

_____

_____

_____

Questions for Discussion

1 Why do you believe young people take drugs?
2 In recent times parents have published pictures of their dead children to warn other teens of the dangers of taking drugs. Do you think these shock tactics work? Is this a good way to deter young people from taking drugs?

Heroin: The Realities

 ## What is it?

Heroin is sold as a brownish white powder. It is commonly called 'smack', 'H' or 'gear'. It can be smoked, snorted or dissolved, but it's usually injected.

 ## Effects of Using Heroin

When it's injected, heroin produces a rapid rush lasting less than a minute. Then the user begins to feel drowsy and peaceful and may feel detached from the real world. When a person is using regularly the level of the drug in the body increases, and they will need to take heroin every four to six hours to avoid withdrawal symptoms – nausea, vomiting, diarrhoea, cramps, sweats, twitching and symptoms similar to a heavy cold.

The euphoric effects seem to be limited to the early stages of a drug-using career: at first the user takes the drug to feel good, but later they need it to feel normal. Once addicted the heroin abuser's primary purpose in life is getting and using the drug.

When heroin is used regularly, the user develops a tolerance. This means they need more heroin to achieve the same intensity or effect. With physical dependence, the body adapts to the presence of the drug and withdrawal symptoms may occur if use is reduced or stopped. Heroin is physically and emotionally highly addictive.

Because heroin users do not know the actual strength of the drug or its true contents, they are at risk of overdose or death. Sharing needles carries a greater risk of infection with HIV, AIDS and hepatitis. (Source: www.mqi.ie)

What is heroin and how is it taken?

_____

_____

Is heroin addictive?

_____

_____

What are the effects of using heroin?

_____

_____

What happens to heroin users in the later stages of drug use?

_____

_____

What implications does this addiction have for the person taking the drug?

_____

_____

Heroin

```
K  K  W  A  Y  H  S  B  M  K  Q  S  H  M  X
S  S  E  L  E  M  O  H  P  B  M  I  L  H  R
M  E  Y  C  J  L  C  I  D  M  N  W  J  M  V
I  J  I  V  Y  A  Y  V  V  S  A  W  T  X  M
M  J  R  T  D  W  C  Y  S  W  O  R  D  X  N
E  Q  A  H  I  A  C  E  V  M  P  E  W  R  Z
T  V  R  Q  N  R  L  T  C  N  A  S  Y  C  Y
H  N  I  J  J  D  U  P  M  Z  E  C  T  J  N
A  F  A  T  E  H  S  P  F  I  P  P  K  C  I
D  U  N  E  C  T  Y  C  M  X  E  A  U  G  J
O  J  N  V  T  I  M  G  D  I  Z  C  E  I  S
N  H  U  G  E  W  D  Y  X  J  P  V  M  Z  T
E  R  G  A  D  I  C  D  P  X  X  U  J  G  H
U  N  P  Z  X  X  N  P  A  U  I  E  J  D  L
Q  W  C  N  Q  I  R  S  F  R  F  G  U  E  H
```

ADDICTIVE	DROWSY	HIV
HOMELESS	IMPURITIES	INJECTED
METHADONE	NEEDLES	SMACK
VEINS	WITHDRAWAL	

 # Role Play

This role play is designed to explore the lives of two people. One of them is suffering the effects of peer pressure to take cannabis. The role play will require three characters: John; Mary, John's girlfriend; and Annie, the talkshow host.

Annie: 'Welcome to *Ask Annie!* Today's guests are Mary and John. Mary is a fifteen-year-old girl from the south of Ireland. She's here today to tell us her story and to ask for our help. This is Mary's story.'

Mary: has been going out with John for a few years now. He smokes cannabis fairly regularly. She is often in his company when he smokes with friends and, even though she has no interest in taking drugs, she does feel under pressure when a joint is passed around. Lately Mary has found out that John has been using heroin. She is afraid to talk to him about this. Mary has seen a huge change in John's personality and now she is concerned that his drug problem is getting out of control.

John: sees his drug taking as no big deal. He thinks Mary should chill out and not take things so seriously.

Annie: 'Audience, what do you think?'

Questions for Discussion

1 What should Mary do?
2 What do you think is worrying her?
3 Why is Mary staying in this relationship?
4 How can she improve her situation? What are her options?
5 What do you think will happen if she stays with John?

Drug Poems

An acrostic poem is a poem in which the first letter of each line spells out the theme of the poem.

In this topic you're going to write your own poem in an acrostic style. The following example shows how an acrostic poem looks. Work in pairs to come up with your own acrostic poem about ecstasy or heroin. If you like, you could include some or all of the words from the wordsearches earlier in this chapter.

Here's an example:

Drugs
Danger and devastation enter your life,
Real life departs and selfishness is rife,
Under the influence you fail to see,
Grave danger ahead of ye,
So think carefully, my friend, for your future is near and dear.

The story of an addict

'Robert grew up in a small town where nothing much out of the ordinary ever happened. He was talented at art and was doing well at school. But he was quiet and he didn't really feel like he fitted in with the other kids. His first experience of drugs was a shared joint of cannabis at a friend's house. At first he was unsure but, not wanting to seem boring, he gave in. No one forced him but it made him feel part of the group.

'Soon Robert was taking cannabis regularly and by the time he was sixteen, bored with cannabis, he began taking speed. His first experience with speed was a bit scary. Before long, though, it had become part of his life. Robert believes that his drug use held him back at school. Nights out taking ecstasy took their toll on Robert's concentration. When he left school he got a job at a local chemist. There he became friendly with another assistant – he too was a drug user.

'Before long Robert was stealing prescription drugs from the pharmacy as well as stealing from his family to fund his ever-growing drug habit. It was during this period that drugs really became a way of life for him. "We had a drug for every occasion and a remedy for every effect. We'd take speed at night for clubbing, then sleepers for bed and perhaps a bit of speed to get us going for breakfast. Sometimes we would swap the pharmacy drugs for street drugs."

'After about a year of habitual use, Robert lost his job in the chemist and decided to move to Dublin. He was soon involved in the drug scene there. It was then that he lost touch with his family and began to lose control.

'"I began to feel paranoid. I constantly thought that I was been followed and I'd literally dive into street doorways and peek out to check who was following me. This really scared me to death. Everyone around me seemed to be going too far. I hated to see people I knew changing as one after the other got into heroin. I felt so alone. I wanted to give up, but I knew giving up meant detaching myself from the only friends I knew, returning home and admitting my problem to my parents. I knew that would bring shame on my family but I hoped that they would stand by me and thankfully they did.

'"I am so lucky that I did not get a police record or any long-term health problems. The first few months back at home were hard, but slowly I began to build my confidence. I made new friends and I even enrolled in art college. Suddenly the future is looking bright again, I will take one day at a time."'

(Adapted from users' stories, www.channel4.com

Why do you think Robert started taking drugs? What were the effects of his drug use (e.g. on relationships, career, etc.)?

_____

_____

_____

Robert claims he was 'so lucky'. Why? What could have happened to him?

_____

_____

_____

Why do you think he used so many different drugs?

_____

_____

_____

If you knew someone who had a drug problem, what could you do?

_____

_____

_____

Drug Project

In groups research a particular drug. Present your findings to the rest of your class. Choose whatever method of presentation you think is most appropriate. Here are some of the things you should think about.

- The name of the drug and pictures of the drug.
- What highs do users get from the drug?
- What lows does it cause?
- The long-term effects of using.
- The effects on society.

For your last section you could cover one of the following:

- a user's story
- rehabilitation services
- important facts about the drug
- who is at risk.

Helpful Websites

www.mqi.ie
www.nida.nih.gov
www.teens.drugabuse.gov

Name that Drug Crossword

Across

3 _____ use can cause HIV and AIDS through sharing needles

5 Available as resin, grass or oil

7 Found on blotting paper with designs on it

9 One of the most commonly used drugs

11 Makes cigarettes highly addictive

12 Taken to improve athletes' performance

Down

1 Similar to when you drive fast

2 Prescribed by the doctor – but users may become dependent

4 Associated with the club scene

6 These grow in the wild and can be dried and eaten

8 You might use this in the morning to kick start your day, or when you meet a friend.

10 Comes in a powder and is usually snorted up the nose

13 These aren't normally classed as drugs; they can be found in most households

Module Review

Date:

In this module I learned about: _____

I enjoyed this module because: _____

I disliked this module because: _____

I would rate this module __ out of ten for relevance to my life. This module was relevant/not relevant to my life because:

_____

_____

_____

Module 10

Personal Safety

 Are you a Risk Taker?

Try this questionnaire:

1	Is there a smoke alarm in your home?	Yes	No
2	Do you wear a seat belt in the car?	Yes	No
3	Do you wear a cycling helmet?	Yes	No
4	If you were in a car with someone who was driving too fast, would you: a) ask them to slow down? b) say nothing?		
5	Do you always wait for the traffic lights to change before crossing the road?	Yes	No
6	Would you give your mobile number to a complete stranger?	Yes	No
7	Would you agree to physically meet someone you met in a chat room on the Internet?	Yes	No
8	Would you be prepared to get into a car if you thought the driver had been drinking?	Yes	No
9	Would you take an illegal drug from someone if you found your friends were trying it out?	Yes	No
10	Would you be prepared to walk home late at night on your own?	Yes	No
11	Would you ask your parents or another adult for advice on how you could make better decisions on things that worry you?	Yes	No

If you answered 'no' to most of questions 1–5 above and 'yes' to most of questions 6–10 you need to be more careful about your personal safety.

 **Help Agencies**

 **Personal**

Sometimes people with problems can contact agencies, services or individuals to help them. Get together in groups and make a list of agencies you already know about. Some examples have been done for you.

Listens to Children
1800 666 666

Agency/Service/Individual	Support for
Cura	Unplanned pregnancy
Childline	Crisis line for children in trouble or danger
Bodywhys	People with eating disorders

Weekly Task

Find the name, address and telephone number of the local branches of some of the help agencies listed above.

Help for	Agency	Address	Telephone

Class Task

Design a card for a specific help agency. It should include the name, address, phone number and description of the advice they give. Each student can stick their card to a poster for everyone to see.

Recognising Unsafe Situations

 ## Road Deaths

Questions for Discussion

1 Why do you think so many young people are involved in car accidents?
2 Do you think young people risk their lives in cars? Why?
3 What has been done to reduce road deaths? Is this effective?
4 What do you think can be done to reduce the number of fatalities on Irish roads?

Write an acrostic poem using the letters of the word 'speeding'.
Here are some words and phrases you could think about including:

tragedy	driver	suffering
carnage	passengers	pain
speed	drugs and alcohol	pointless
emergency services	reckless	teenagers
young lives	guards	careless

S _____

P _____

E _____

E _____

D _____

I _____

N _____

G _____

How do you feel when you see roady safety advertisements that show death and destruction?

_____

_____

_____

Do you think they are effective? Why/why not?

_____

_____

_____

Do you think some of the images are too graphic?

_____

_____

_____

 # Role Play

Mary and Claire have been for a night out with friends. After the disco Mary's boyfriend offers them both a lift home. Claire can't be sure but she thinks he has been drinking. Mary wants to take the lift and is trying to persuade Claire to come with her. Claire has to try resist Mary's persuasion and not take the lift.

Group Discussion
1   What are the dangers of taking this lift?
2   Would you take the lift? Why/why not?
3   What is an alternative option for Claire?

Personal Work
Think of a situation in which you felt at risk. Could you have avoided this situation?

→ Joyriding

Joyriding is a big problem in Ireland. Despite the tragic effects of their activities, some teenagers remain undeterred.

Read the following headlines and then discuss the questions that follow.

Joyriders kill two guards

Taxi driver dies in smash

Joyriders hit canal bank project

Joyriders' burned-out cars destroy city beauty spot

Seven-year-old girl killed in hit and run

Two teenage friends die – hit by stolen car after night out

Man dies after collision with stolen car

How do you feel when you read articles like these in the papers?

_____

_____

_____

Do you believe joyriding is still a problem in towns/cities in Ireland?

_____

_____

Why do you think young people risk their lives by joyriding?

_____

_____

_____

What do you think should be done to tackle the problem of joyriding?

_____

_____

_____

Violence

We live in an increasingly violent society. Below are some headlines reporting the types of crime that are becoming familiar in everyday news stories.

Man brutally attacked for mobile phone

Vicious knife attack

Family home destroyed in arson attack

Teenager raped and beaten in savage attack

Three die following head-on collision with joyriders

Young teenager suffers severe head injuries after night club brawl

Briefly discuss the following questions in groups and then as a class.

1 Why do you think there has been such an increase in crime in recent years?
2 Can you think of examples of other violent crimes against individuals?
3 Have you heard of any attacks or violent crimes in your own area?
4 How do you think crime affects the morale/image of a community?
5 Do you think the prison system in Ireland works? Is there another alternative?
6 What, in your opinion, could be done to reduce teenage crime?

Weekly Task

Look through the newspaper (ideally more than one paper) and bring in crime-related articles for discussion in class.

 Media and Violence

Think of some violent images you have seen on television lately. Who was the violence directed at? _____

Do you think violent imagery is necessary on television? Give reasons.

_____

_____

Do you think violent images on television contribute to violent behaviour in society? Discuss.

_____

_____

What do you think could be done to reduce teenage exposure to violent imagery?

_____

_____

A bottle broken across someone's head. A man jumping through a glass window and remaining unscathed. These are unrealistic images of violence often seen on our television screens. The reality is death or serious injury. Do you think such images influence violence in society?

_____

_____

 Personal Safety

Here are some situations in which people find themselves at risk. Do you think these people realised that they were putting themselves in a dangerous situation?

Teenage girl attacked and raped

'A 17-year-old girl was attacked and raped after leaving a night club in the capital last night. The victim was alone at the time of the attack. She had left her friends minutes earlier to get a taxi home. At approximately 2.30, a man wielding a knife grabbed the girl and dragged her down an alleyway. She is presently recovering in hospital.'

How could this teenager have avoided being attacked?

_____

_____

_____

Why do you think she left her friends?

_____

_____

_____

_____

Do you think alcohol influenced her decision that night?

_____

_____

_____

Would you walk alone in your area at night?

_____

_____

_____

Fears grow for missing girl

'A distraught mother has made a heartfelt appeal to anyone with information on the whereabouts of her daughter to come forward. Mary Lewis has not seen her daughter Claire since Tuesday evening. As the days pass, Claire's family are becoming increasingly apprehensive. Claire had told friends she planned to meet a guy she had been chatting to in an internet chat room.'

What do you think might have happened to Claire?

_____

_____

_____

What should Claire have done if she planned to meet this guy?

_____

_____

_____

What are the dangers of using internet chat rooms?

_____

_____

_____

How can you make sure you are safe when using the internet?

_____

_____

_____

Why is it important to be safe when using the internet?

_____

_____

Two teenagers drink poison at bonfire

'Two boys are recovering in hospital after consuming what they believed was alcohol at a bonfire last night. The boys were drinking with friends when a vodka bottle was passed around. The youths drank from the bottle but quickly became violently ill. They were rushed to hospital where their condition is described as critical.'

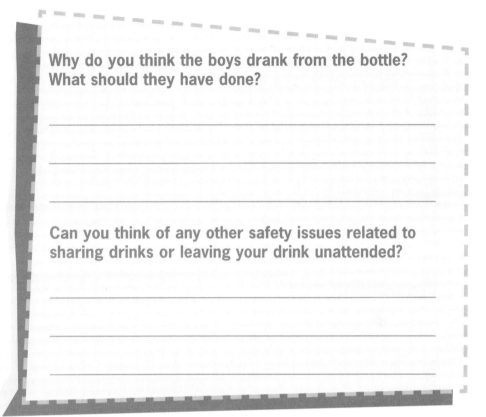

Why do you think the boys drank from the bottle? What should they have done?

_____

_____

_____

Can you think of any other safety issues related to sharing drinks or leaving your drink unattended?

_____

_____

_____

 ## Safety Case Studies

Read the case studies below. What you would do in each situation? Bear in mind how your actions could affect your personal safety.

You have a test tomorrow but you know you have not studied for it. You have failed the last two tests and you don't want to fail another one. Your friend rings you and asks if you want to skip school with him tomorrow. He knows a good place to go.

What would you do? Why? Is this the responsible and right thing to do?

_____

_____

What are the risks to your personal safety?

_____

_____

You're leaving school later than normal because you were studying late. You want to get home as quickly as possible. You take a short cut through the back of your housing estate. As you enter the estate you notice a man following you.

What should you do?

_____

_____

What should you not do?

_____

_____

You are at a disco with your friends. When the disco finishes you have to get a taxi to the opposite side of town. You say goodbye to your friends and walk to get a taxi even though your parents have told you not to be out on your own late at night.

What might happen in this situation?

_____

_____

What could you do to avoid getting separated from your friends?

_____

_____

You are drinking for the first time. Your parents have no idea where you are. While you are drinking a row breaks out among some of the boys and it is getting violent. One of the boys throws a rock through a car window. You are very scared and don't want to get involved or be wrongly accused, but you are a good 30-minute walk from home.

What should you do?

_____

_____

What should you not do?

_____

_____

Should she stay or should she go?

Denise has been going out with her boyfriend Luke for a few months. They were out together one night and Luke was drinking. On their way home Denise and Luke had a disagreement because he spoke to his ex-girlfriend at the disco. Luke got so angry with Denise that he lost his temper and hit her. He apologised straightaway, and has never been violent before, so Denise is willing to give him a second chance. She feels she is partly to blame because she provoked him.

Why do think Denise is giving Luke a second chance?

_____

_____

Do you think she is right?

_____

_____

What should Denise do? Who should she tell? Who could she talk to?

_____

_____

Do you think Denise is putting herself at risk in this relationship?

_____

_____

Who could she go to for advice?

_____

_____

BUS

Having fun or causing havoc? Mark's story

'I just recently moved to a new estate. I had no friends at first but recently I have met new people. We usually just hang around the estate in groups. Sometimes we drink but mainly we just hang out. It's a good laugh, slagging people passing and rising the old ones. The neighbours get really annoyed with us and sometimes they call the guards, but they can't do anything. Some of the lads have damaged property and painted graffiti on the walls. I think the neighbours should just chill out.'

Do you think this gang is intimidating? Why?

_____

_____

Why are the neighbours upset?

_____

_____

What could happen to Mark if he continues to hang out with this group?

_____

_____

Have you ever been intimidated by a gang? How?

_____

_____

Gangs

Do you think people's behaviour can be influenced by being in a group? How?

_____

_____

Do you think the behaviours listed below could be influenced by a group of friends? Describe how.

Drinking alcohol/smoking.

_____

_____

The language you use.

_____

_____

What you say about others.

_____

_____

Believing you'll get away with something.

_____

_____

Helpful Websites

www.business2000.ie/cases
www.mindbodysoul.gov.uk/safety
www.news.bbc.co.uk/cbbcnews

Module Review

Date:

In this module I learned about: _____

I enjoyed this module because: _____

I disliked this module because: _____

I would rate this module __ out of ten for relevance to my life. This module was relevant/not relevant to my life because:

_____

_____

_____

Crossword Solutions

 **Healthy Eating Crossword**

Across
2 Fast
3 Pasta
8 Cholesterol
9 Organic
12 Grilled
14 Oranges
15 Anaemia

Down
1 Malnutrition
4 Diabetes
5 Fibre
6 Calories
7 Protein
8 Calcium
10 Steam
11 Eggs
13 Fats

 # Exercise Crossword

Across

6 Carbohydrates
8 Endorphins
9 Yoga
10 Thirty
11 Water
13 Time

Down

1 Aerobics
2 Stretching
3 Increases
4 Jogging
5 Strength
7 Burnout
12 Rest

Name That Drug Crossword

Across

  3 Heroin
  5 Cannabis
  7 Acid
  9 Alcohol
 11 Nicotine
 12 Steroids

Down

  1 Speed
  2 Tranquillisers
  4 Ecstasy
  6 Magic mushrooms
  8 Caffeine
 10 Cocaine
 13 Solvents